THE RICH SINGLE LIFE

ABUNDANCE, OPPORTUNITY & PURPOSE IN GOD

ANDREW FARMER

EDITOR: KEVIN MEATH

PURSUIT OF GODLINESS
SERIES
PDI
COMMUNICATIONS

PDI Communications is a division of PDI Ministries,
which serves a growing network of local churches in
the United States and abroad. For information about
the ministry or for permission to reproduce portions
of this book, please contact us.

PDI Communications
7881 Beechcraft Avenue, Suite B
Gaithersburg, MD 20879

1-800-736-2202
fax: 301-948-7833
pdi@pdinet.org
www.pdinet.org

THE RICH SINGLE LIFE

Author: Andrew Farmer
Cover design: Gallison Design
Cover photos: Rich Genders
Cover and book layout: Martin Stanley

ISBN 1-881039-07-2

Printed in the United States of America

0799

The cover photos for this book were taken of single Christians, each a member of a local church
affiliated with PDI Ministries.

FOREWORD by JOSHUA HARRIS

A friend recently gave me a humorous greeting card. The front read, "I'm thinking of starting a new support group: Non-Daters Anonymous." On the inside was written "Meetings will be held Friday and Saturday night. B.Y.O.C." (Bring Your Own Chocolate) I laughed when I read it, but was saddened by the not-so-subtle message. Singleness, this card was saying, is something to grieve over. We should weep, feel sorry for ourselves, and attempt to drown out the pain in twice-weekly feasts of fudge.

In a day when singleness is often viewed by Christians and non-Christians alike as if it were an empty bus station in the middle of nowhere, the biblical teaching that any season of singleness is a gift from God can sound ridiculous. "Singleness is a gift? Did you save the receipt?!"

I'm excited to introduce this book because it is decidedly not a "Bring Your Own Chocolate" pity-party. Andy Farmer skillfully shows singles what a valuable opportunity they have. Single Christian men and women are to take full advantage of singleness, not devise ways to escape it.

The Rich Single Life is going to help you for two important reasons. First, it's soaked in Scripture. Its starting point isn't merely the author's experience or lots of testimonies and stories (though you'll find some of both). Instead, he's drawing truth from the Bible and helping us apply that truth to our lives.

Second, and most refreshingly, this book doesn't encourage you to find your identity in your singleness. Thank God! The last thing the world needs is another book that makes singles feel more isolated and dissatisfied, as if we were a separate species of humanity. *The Rich Single Life* will help you see yourself as God sees you—as his child who, by his grace that strengthens you, can do all things.

Finally, Andy's insights will help you find contentment by giving you perspective—God's perspective. Remember, true contentment doesn't hinge on getting what we think will bring happiness. Someone has said, "Contentment is not the fulfillment of what you want, but the realization of how much you already have." It's true. Whether you're nineteen and single or fifty-five and single, or whether you've known the trauma of divorce or the challenges of being a single parent, remember that contentment is a state of trust before God, not a destination at which we may one day arrive. When we focus on a destination (getting married, having kids, owning a home, etc.) as the source of our contentment, it never arrives, because we're always looking for it somewhere off in the future.

I believe the truths contained in this book could revolutionize people's understanding of singleness. Then our motto could be "S.I.A.G." — "Singleness Is A Gift." By God's grace, let's enjoy it to the fullest. Someone has said, "You don't need to do something about your singleness, you need to do something *with* it."

The book you're holding will help you "do something with" your singleness. And this "something" will not only bring rich experience. It will bring glory to God.

June, 1998

HOW TO USE THIS BOOK

The Rich Single Life is part of PDI Communications' Pursuit of Godliness book series designed for group and individual study. The series is the logical outgrowth of four deeply held convictions:

■ The Bible is our infallible standard for faith, doctrine, and practice. Those who resist its authority will be blown off course by their own feelings and cultural trends.

■ Knowledge without application is lifeless. In order to be transformed, we must apply and practice the truth of God's Word in daily life.

■ Application of these principles is impossible apart from the Holy Spirit. While we must participate in change, he is the source of our power.

■ The church is God's intended context for change. God never intended for us to live isolated from or independent of other Christians. Through committed participation in the local church, we find instruction, encouragement, correction, and opportunities to press on toward maturity in Christ.

With the possible exception of the "Group Discussion" questions, the format of this book is equally suited for individuals and small groups. A variety of different elements have been included to make each study as interesting and helpful as possible.

Bible Study: Begin by digging into God's Word. Unless otherwise noted, all Scripture quotations come from the New International Version (NIV) of the Bible.

Warm-Up: A little mental exercise to get you in the mood.

Personal Study: Here is the meat of the lesson, spiced with occasional questions to help you apply what you're reading.

Margin Questions: If you have the time, dig deeper into the lesson as you *Meditate On...* biblical truths or turn to related passages *For Further Study*.

Group Discussion: Though you may not get past the first question or two, these are guaranteed to get your group thinking and talking about real-life issues.

Recommended Reading: For those who want to learn more about a particular topic, suggested resources are listed at the end of each study.

Group discussion will be better served when members work through the material in advance. If you aren't able to cover a study thoroughly in one meeting, feel free to split it up. And remember that you're not going through this book alone. The Holy Spirit is your tutor. With his help, these studies have the potential to change your life. ■

CONTENTS

AN EXCELLENT INVESTMENT

BIBLE STUDY 1 Corinthians 7:32-35

WARM-UP Someone once said the English and Americans are two peoples separated by a common language. Even in the United States we have different words for the same thing, depending on the region of the country you are in. Match the following carbonated-beverage names with the region where you will most likely hear it.

Term	Region
____ soda	1. Southeast
____ soft drink	2. Midwest
____ coke	3. Northeast
____ pop	4. West

(See page 14 for answers)

PERSONAL STUDY "You're not from around here, are you?" With those words, I knew I had been exposed. My southern drawl had given me away again.

Born and raised in the deep South, I had moved to Philadelphia in response to what I had sensed was God's leading. But the more I tried to adapt to northern ways, the more I wondered whether it was God's wisdom or his sense of humor that had been at work in moving me here.

I didn't know it would be such a big adjustment. It's not like I'd left the country or anything, but there was a world of difference. Besides the weather being colder, the pace of life is much faster—in Philadelphia, a yellow light at the intersection doesn't mean "caution," it means "speed up." And while it's a great place to live, I still haven't mastered the language. None of my best words, like "y'all," really work here. After a great meal at a friend's house one evening, I let loose with a southerner's highest and most genuine after-dinner compliment: "Boy, I'm full as a tick." They didn't even offer me dessert.

It's been 17 years now, and I'm still a hick in the 'hood. Have I adapted? I'd like to think so. Do I feel at home? Not entirely. I've learned that no matter how much I try to blend in, I'll always be a transplant, someone who resides in a culture not ultimately his own. I live in Yankee country, but I'll never be a Yankee.

So what does my little cross-cultural odyssey have to do with being a single adult?

As I interact with my single friends, they often describe a similar feeling of dislocation. There is a vague but consistent sense that they are single in a married person's world. Most would not say they feel discriminated against or looked down upon, but simply misunderstood. In the same way that I cannot as a southerner expect my northern community to adjust to my way of doing things, in the cross-cultural interaction between single folk and married, singles usually end up doing most of the adapting. Now this would be understandable if we were to consider that, historically, "singles" (as we define them today) made up only about 3 percent of the population.[1] Yet a number of trends, such as a steady 50 percent divorce rate, have been swelling the number of singles in our society at an amazing rate. Many now forecast that single adults will make up half the adult population by the early part of the next century.

An explosion of singleness in the past 50 years has emerged largely from a redesignation of singleness as a respectable lifestyle. In 1957, for example, more than half of the U.S. population viewed singleness as something "sick" and "immoral." By 1991, just 34 years later, more than half the population had come to feel there was simply no good reason to get married![2]

Despite what pollsters may tell us about the present-day acceptability of singleness, on a real-life level it is still widely seen as a problem that needs to be solved, escaped from, or avoided. Many, if not most, single people still see mar-

Meditate on Leviticus 19:33-34.
If you find someone not like you in your midst, how should you treat him?

> **❝** We tend to think of families as a standard from which we have deviated; their lives are the reality, ours the imitation, the variant, the makeshift. Instead of reshaping our own ways of living, we cobble them together loosely, make do, and perhaps unconsciously, wait to be rescued from our islands and received into the real world.[3] **❞**
>
> **— Barbara Holland**

riage as by far the socially superior state of life. For them, singleness is a place, but marriage is the destination.

---

1 List some differences in the ways single people and married people relate to the following life events.

Christmas holidays:

Vacations:

Grocery shopping:

Weekends:

I experienced the power of this perception recently while attending my 20th high school reunion. Having seen almost no one from high school since graduation day, I was in for a real eye-opener.

As I walked into the ballroom I was struck by two thoughts: "I don't recognize *anyone*," and "I always thought I was much taller than I seem to be now." Then I remembered; I spent most of high school wearing two-inch platform shoes! Anyway, I soon began to recognize people—after making mental adjustments for extra weight and less hair—and was able to reacquaint myself with some old pals.

You know what stood out most to me? I don't mean to sound like a sociology professor, but this is the best way to put it: there was a direct correlation between marital status and level of self-disclosure. Without exception, folks who were married were happy to talk about themselves and what was going on in their lives—and they had lots to say. Yet in talking with people who were single, whether divorced or never married, it seemed they were almost apologetic for their status, and tended to say very little about their personal lives. It was as if these folks felt like second-class citizens at their own reunion.

Writer Barbara Holland, a single woman, laments this sense of inadequacy. "Happily-ever-after has rejected us. The fairy story has spit us out as unworthy, and sometimes we suppose perhaps we are."[4]

For Further Study:
Read 1 Corinthians 2:1-5. When Paul came to the Corinthians, what kind of reputation did he want to leave with them?

3

Have you struggled with thoughts of inadequacy and alienation in your season of singleness? Do you feel like a foreigner in the Kingdom of Marriage and Family? Do you wonder whether you have somehow been misplaced in God's plan?

If you wrestle with your singleness, read on. There is a single life for the Christian that is full of purpose, vitality, and adventure. God has not overlooked you. He isn't waiting for you to get your act together before he will direct your steps, and he isn't playing guessing games with your marital future. He has a place and a plan for you in your singleness. He has a vital and significant role for you to play in his purpose. God has supplied you with an identity that both transcends singleness and enables you to embrace and benefit richly from this time, for as long as it might last. This identity is revealed in God's Word.

Let's begin to explore his plan together by examining a biblical view of singleness.

The Old Testament Reality

Before surveying the Christian view of singleness, we must establish a reference point in the Old Testament. Frankly, for the single person, the Old Testament world was not terribly promising. Family in the ancient world was the primary economic and social foundation. To be single and older than about age 20 was to be effectively cut off from society's benefits. It was the prostitutes, slaves, and beggars who were the "singles" of that day. If some today advocate the "live fast, die young, leave a good-looking corpse" philosophy, the ancient world's approach was more like "marry fast, die young, leave a good-looking family."

For Further Study:
Read Hebrews 11:8-12. What obstacles did Abraham have to overcome in order to exercise his faith in God's promise?

The story of the Old Testament is one of God Almighty expressing his unmerited love to sinners. The Old Testament unfolding of God's plan for a rebellious human race took the form of a promise to a man, Abraham, "to be your God and the God of your descendants after you" (Gen 17:6-7). From this family line would come the ultimate expression of God's love—Jesus the Messiah. So to the already strong social and economic component of the ancient family was added, in the promise of Christ, a vital spiritual component.

Throughout Old Testament Hebrew culture, women were generally married during their teen years. While it was rare for a man in his twenties not to be head of his

4

own household, there are some notable exceptions. Jeremiah (Jer 16:2) and Ezekiel (a widower; Eze 24:8) were two major prophets who apparently remained single throughout most or all of their lives. A quick look at their job descriptions as prophets of doom, however, is sobering for even the most stout-hearted single man. Rahab (the harlot) is also honored in the Bible, but wouldn't exactly provide the best vocational role model for single women (Heb 11:31). Generally, for the typical single individual in Old Testament Hebrew culture, your only hope was marriage, or, if you were male, the alternative hope that you might be gloriously smitten on the front lines of a battle.

The New Testament Hope

Before discouragement sets in too deeply and we're tempted to scurry off to the bookstore for self-help guides and romance novels, let us consider one important fact: there is a second half to the Bible! It is called the New Testament, and we can't fully understand Old Testament realities without reference to it. You see, the Old Testament truths are not stand-alone truths. They are preparatory realities for the great work of redemption in the Cross of Jesus Christ. And this work of the Cross is so profound and pervasive that it will radically alter who we are and what life means to us.

One of the beautiful aspects of the work of Jesus on the Cross is the "ministry of reconciliation" (2Co 5:18-19), whereby sinful man is reconciled to a Holy God. Through his death on the Cross, Jesus overcame our separation from God due to our sin, and brought us into a fellowship with our Creator that is intimate, ongoing, and life-changing. Through the ministry of reconciliation, Christ has also redrawn the lines of social interaction in very benevolent places. With the dawn of the age of redemption in Christ, Old Testament identities—man and woman, Jew and Gentile, married and single—are not abolished, but they are redefined in light of the Cross. All Christians now stand equal before God. All can please God within the context of these fundamental identities. All can enjoy fellowship with God in equal measure and access.

> ❝ In the Christian theology of history, the death of Christ is the central point in history; here all the roads of the past converge; hence all the roads of the future diverge.[5] ❞
>
> — **Stephen Neill**

2 Besides marital status, can you think of any other Old Testament realities that must be understood in light of the New Testament truth of the Cross of Christ? Write them in the space below.

Meditate on Colossians 3:1-11.
How can we "set our minds on things above"? Why should we?

For the single adult, this radical new reality offers itself boldly in the person of Jesus himself. When we realize a little of what it meant to be single in ancient Hebrew society, how amazing it is that God would come to earth and carry out his entire earthly ministry as a single man! Setting aside the thorny theological questions of marriage and the Godhead, how it must have perplexed the Jews of his day to have this Rabbi, this leader of multitudes, be a single man.

Not only that, but Jesus seemed to have a particular place in his heart for single men and women, many of whom he counted as his closest friends. It is almost certain that at least a few of his chosen disciples were single during his earthly ministry. Also, Mary, Martha, and Lazarus were apparently single siblings who might have been oddities in the community but were close with the Savior. And Jesus' interaction with the multi-divorced Samaritan woman at the well (John 4) was a taboo-buster on several fronts.

(There is also a compelling case to be made for the single status of John the Baptist—although if he was married, one can only admire the fortitude of his wife, for whom locusts, honey, and unfashionable clothes must have lost their novelty at some point.)

In the book of Acts we encounter Paul the Apostle, a man whose single status is clearly established in his first letter to the Corinthian church. If we also make the fair assumption that the Apostle John was a widower in the latter years of his ministry, then nearly half the New Testament was either spoken or written by single people!

For Further Study:
Read John 4:1-26. Jesus reached out to a single woman across many barriers. List the important things he told her.

In addition, while it is clear Peter was married (Mk 1:30; 1Co 9:5), scholars believe that a number of Paul's helpers and fellow leaders (including his "son in the faith"

Timothy) may have been single for significant portions of their ministry. Very possibly, the well-commended church at Philippi would not have been started without the involvement of two apparently single women: Lydia (a successful merchant, whose conversion is recounted in Acts 16:14) and an unnamed slave girl/former demoniac-for-profit (who may well have been converted in association with the events of Acts 16:16-18).

The New Testament example of the vital place of singles in God's plan could not be more clear.

A New Testament Theology of Singleness

Having seen the biblical *example*, what is the biblical *teaching* about singleness? The most significant discussion of singleness in the Bible occurs in Paul's first letter to the Corinthian church. This church had been established in a wild, pagan party town. Consequently, new believers were coming into the church with all manner of what we might call "creative living arrangements." In 1 Corinthians 7, Paul settles a dispute by addressing at length the relative spirituality of marriage and singleness. You see, while some of the Corinthian Christians had been arguing that any unmarried adult must be some shade of weird, others were boasting that marriage was for people who weren't really serious about "giving it all for God." Some of this latter group were even married folks whose main motivation was to escape their marriage responsibilities.

> **❝** A key issue for Christian theology is what emphasis to give to singleness in relation to the state of marriage. Is it to be treated as pathological: something abnormal that requires either a cure or at least the alleviation of pain? Or should we emphasize it as a privilege: the special vocation of the truly devoted follower of Christ? The middle way is to view singleness and marriage as parallel states, each having their own particular joys and sorrows.[6] **❞**
>
> — **V.M. Sinton**

For Further Study:
Read Matthew 19:1-12. Eunuchs (celibates, in effect) were excluded from the community of Israel. In this teaching, how does Jesus affirm those who are not married?

Where does Paul come down in this debate? That marriage is not the "superior" state, nor is it a concession to those without the "superior" gift of celibacy. Singleness is neither the highest form of spirituality nor the unfortunate status of the unmarried. As Paul graciously responds to these confused folks, he lays out the following fundamental principles.

The sovereign hand of God has placed each of his children in his or her present status. "As the Lord has assigned to each one, as God has called each, in this manner let him walk" (v. 17, NAS). In this verse, Paul is putting a freeze on a sudden frenzy of marriages, divorces, and remarriages that had broken out among these young Corinthian believers as they tried practically, although unwisely, to walk out their new faith. But on a deeper level, Paul is pointing them to the providence of God—that is, they are exactly where God wants them to be at this time. It's Paul's way of saying, "Relax, God is in control."

---

3 In addressing the issue of marriage and singleness in 1 Corinthians 7, Paul is trying to get people to adopt a "wartime mentality" (vv. 29-31). How can this wartime mentality be reflected in the following areas?

Career:

Friendships:

Money:

Free time:

With God's providential positioning comes supernatural enabling. "But each man has his own gift (literally 'charismata') from God" (v. 7). Are you a charismatic? If you're single you are. If you get married you'll still be. Paul says that there is a gift—a "charismata" or supernatural ability—to live the life to which you have been called. You'll have the gift of singleness as long as you are single. When you get married, you won't need it anymore. As Elisabeth Elliot has written,

> It is within the sphere of the circumstances He chooses for us—single, married, widowed—that we receive Him. It is there and nowhere else that He makes Himself known to us. It is there that we are allowed to serve Him....Single life may be only a stage of a life's journey, but even a stage is a gift. God may replace it with another gift, but the receiver accepts His gifts with thanksgiving. *This* gift for *this* day.[7]

**Meditate on
2 Timothy 2:1.** How
can you be strong in
the grace of your
singleness?

**Our view of our present situation should be shaped by
eternal perspective.** "What I mean, brothers, is that the
time is short....For this world in its present form is passing away" (1Co 7:29, 31). Paul urges us to live in the
ongoing reality that the eternal future is pressing into the
temporal now. He is concerned that we live undistractedly
in joyful anticipation of the approaching kingdom. And he
issues a call to all those who desire to make a difference.
Both singles and marrieds can apply. Paul's advocacy of
singleness ("I wish that all men were even as myself," v7.)
is rooted in a holy practicality that sees the goal and the
best way of getting there.

What concerns us defines us.

I would like you to be free from concern. An unmarried man is concerned about the Lord's affairs—how
he can please the Lord. But a married man is concerned about the affairs of this world—how he can
please his wife—and his interests are divided. An
unmarried woman or
virgin is concerned
about the Lord's
affairs: Her aim is to
be devoted to the Lord
in both body and spir-
it. But a married
woman is concerned
about the affairs of this
world—how she can
please her husband. I
am saying this for your own good, not to restrict
you, but that you may live in a right way *in undivided devotion to the Lord* (1Co 7:32-35).

> ❝ I am not single because I am too
spiritually unstable to possibly deserve a
husband, nor because I am too spiritually
mature to possibly need one. I am single
because God is so abundantly good to me,
because this is his best for me.[8] ❞
> — **Paige Benton**

This "undivided devotion to the Lord" is the essence of
biblical identity for the single adult. It is rooted in the
sovereignty of a God who places people in appropriate situations for the best possible reasons. It is steeped in the
love of a God who uses even the most difficult of situations for the greatest possible benefit. It is sustained by
the wisdom of a God whose timing is perfect and whose
guidance is sure.

You may not live under the present threat of inevitable
persecution for your faith. (Or maybe you do.) Nevertheless,
we all live in "times that are short." If you are a Christian,
don't despise the state to which you have been called. Live
in the gift of your singleness for as long as you have the
gift. And whether or not God ever ordains the prospect of

ONE CHRISTIAN'S UNDIVIDED DEVOTION

The Apostle Paul encourages single people to live in undivided devotion to the Lord (1Co 7:35). What does this really mean? For the past few years, my brother John has explored one form of undivided devotion. He sensed God calling him to disengage from his life routine and pursue the task of feeding the poor. After much prayer, counsel, and preparation over a period of a couple of years, he took an opportunity with a Christian relief organization to serve in famine relief in Africa. This involved selling his home and business, and moving from Texas to a vastly different world. I'll let him tell you about the advantages of singleness during this period of his life.

"I have spent the past five years working in central Africa in post-war refugee situations with a Christian relief and development organization. I am single, and began this work when I was thirty-five years old. I worked in Somalia, Kenya, Angola, and the refugee camps along the Rwandan/Zaire (now Democratic Republic of the Congo) border following the Civil War in Rwanda.

"For several reasons, I can't imagine trying to work in this type of calling and not be a single man. First is the issue of safety. These locations are for the most part officially non-family duty stations—the many international organizations working in these areas allow only their staff members access to the area. Families and visitors are not allowed. Most of these areas were still unstable politically and prone to outbreaks of renewed conflict or banditry. Also, in case of evacuation (which happened several times during my service there), all the organizations are concerned with moving the fewest people possible as quickly as possible. It is not a pro-family work environment.

"Another challenge is stability. The work requires frequent travel and change of duty station. I would live in a location three months on average, then move to another location. While I was able to take rest breaks outside the pressure areas, my home was literally where I placed my bags. Most of our accommodations consisted of team housing—everyone on the relief team in the same house. It certainly isn't a way to live if you are trying to build a home life.

"Finally, it is by definition a very stressful life. Where you work, chaos is the only government, and there are not enough hours in the day to even keep up with the needs that continually pile up around you. Relief work demands a level of attention and commitment that makes the things I was used to in the states—leisure, free time, and privacy—luxuries at best. To carry a daily concern for the safety of a wife and the quality of a marriage would have been overwhelming to me.

"I look forward to the next step in God's plan for my life. It is actually exciting to be able to consider the possibility of marriage someday after five years of it being a non-issue. But I am grateful for the opportunity I have had in Africa and for the gift of singleness that has made it possible."

— **John Farmer**

10

marriage for your life, bring faith for the present and hope for the future, because there is much to be done. Who better to set a hand to the task than you?

Real Solutions for Real Life

This book seeks to apply the truth and the heart of Scripture to the single life in a way that is practical, but not simplistic. Much of today's popular advice to singles is both simplistic and ineffective. It basically tells people just to cope with singleness as cheerfully as possible. And coping *can* seem like an answer to a lot of problems. Coping techniques come in many forms, such as throwing ourselves into careers, or going from one relationship to another looking for Mister/Miss Right. One more example: If your best time is spent in front of the TV or PC, you are probably coping. Coping, you see, is anything we do to pass the time while we wait for life to "really begin."

For Further Study:
Read 2 Corinthians 11:16-33. List the hardships that tested Paul's undivided devotion to the Lord.

But there are big problems with coping. A man once told me, "If the only tool you have in your tool box is a hammer, all your problems will look like nails." Coping can be that kind of tool.

Like a hammer, coping is convenient and requires little training to use. My hammer may help unstick a door, but it won't do a very good job fixing the hard drive on my computer. In fact, I've realized that when I get my hammer out to solve a problem, it's probably because I'm out of real solutions. The same with coping. It's reactive, not creative. It just doesn't deal with the issues of life in useful ways.

Coping won't do. Neither will fantasy, avoidance, nostalgia, diversion, or any other of a host of "one size fits all" tools we might find stashed in the bottom of our life-management tool boxes. We need better tools—solid, versatile, and fit for use by everyone from the novice to the craftsman. This book attempts to provide some of those tools.

The idea of "richness" in the title of this book has to do with substance, a weight and permanence to life that is not devalued by cultural or personal fluctuations. It

> **"** Singleness has been a noble and courageous path...ever since Jesus and the Apostle Paul chose it 'because of the kingdom of heaven'....The courage comes when you sense God calling you to singleness (for this chapter of your life) and you accept the call with zeal and creative planning for His glory.[9] **"**
>
> **— John Piper**

11

has to do with abundance, an overflow that elevates life above the poverty of weakness and loss. It has to do with wherewithal, or purchasing power. The rich single life is not inconsequential; it registers in the marketplace of human existence. It is the precise opposite of coping.

The rich single life is one of investment and return. It requires active wisdom and wise activity to maintain and develop. But as Jesus promises in numerous parables, those who make the right investment will do much more than merely survive. If we plant well, we will harvest. If we manage well, we will be rewarded. If we invest well, we will prosper. This vision is for all believers; it will be applied in this book for single people in particular.

Meditate on Galatians 6:7-10. How can you "sow to please the Spirit" as a single adult?

An Investment Strategy for the Rich Single Life

To take this analogy one step further, let's assert that the "investment goal" for the single adult is to get rich, in the best sense of the word. In order to achieve our investment goal we need a vehicle (banking terminology for things such as CDs, stocks, mutual funds, and the like). The spiritual "investment vehicle" for the single adult is what Paul set out in 1Corinthians 7:35— Undivided Devotion to the Lord. It is a high-risk (in a worldly sense), high-yield tool backed by the eternal decrees and purposes of God himself.

> **"** Prize the advantages you enjoy; know the value of them. Esteem them as highly while you have them, as others do after they have lost them. Pray constantly and fervently for this very thing, that God would teach you to set a due value upon them. And let it be a matter of daily thanksgiving to God, that he has made you a partaker of these benefits. Indeed, the more full and explicit you are herein, the more sensible you will be of the cause you have to be thankful; the more lively conviction you will have of the greatness of the blessing.[10] **"**
>
> — **John Wesley,**
> **from a tract written for single people**

The only thing lacking then is strategy—ways to manage and invest this vehicle of Undivided Devotion for the best possible return. I would like to submit the following mix of investment strategies for your consideration. Each of these eight strategies corresponds to the theme of one of the eight remaining Studies in this book. The strategies are biblically sound and can provide the right mix of short-term protection and long-term growth for any single person's spiritual portfolio.

12

STRATEGIES

Study Two: The rich single life gains identity from recognizing the extent to which God has gone to fill the gap between who we are and what we can be.

Study Three: The rich single life mines the essence of our identity and season of life for the hidden treasures of opportunity.

Study Four: The rich single life develops a faith that roots below the topsoil of culture and circumstance, yielding the fruit of good decisions and a hunger to obey God.

Study Five: The rich single life resonates with the impact of a whole-hearted devotion to God and his agenda for our lives.

Study Six: The rich single life exhibits a love for others that produces meaningful friendships radiating the deep glow of fellowship.

Study Seven: The rich single life is prepared and willing to pursue a relationship toward marriage in submission to God's timing, wisdom, and Word.

Study Eight: The rich single life embraces a biblical vision for marriage with sober but faith-filled anticipation.

Study Nine: The rich single life confronts the universal challenge of loneliness with biblical hope.

Before we proceed, let's keep in mind this sound perspective from Randy Alcorn: "Let me assume the role of 'eternal financial counselor' and offer this advice: choose your investments carefully; compare their rates of interest; consider their ultimate trustworthiness; and especially compare how they will be working for you a few million years from now."[11] ■

GROUP DISCUSSION 1. At what point in life do you think someone becomes a "single adult"?

2. Have you ever been a minority in a cross-cultural situation? What feelings did it produce?

3. If you went to your high school reunion, what would be the first thing you wanted people to know about you? What would be the second?

4. In addition to the testimony from the mission field (see p.10), what are some other situations where being single might be better than being married?

5. What are some ways you have seen God's sovereign hand at work in your life?

6. What are some ways you have experienced the gift of singleness?

7. Are there any ways you tend to think or act which may be attempts just to cope with your singleness? Describe them.

8. What investments of yourself can you be making right now to give you a greater return on your singleness?

RECOMMENDED READING FOR THE SAVVY INVESTOR

Knowing God by J. I. Packer (Downers Grove, IL: InterVarsity Press, 1973)

A Good Start by Charles Haddon Spurgeon (Morgan, PA: Soli Deo Gloria Publications, 1995)

A Singular Devotion: 366 Portraits of Singles Who Have Changed the World by Harold Ivan Smith (New York, NY: Fleming H. Revell, 1990)

Answers to Warm-Up
(from page 1):
Soda (Northeast)
Soft Drink (West)
Coke (Southeast)
Pop (Midwest)

RICH IN IDENTITY

Strategy: The rich single life gains identity from recognizing the extent to which God has gone to fill the gap between who we are and what we can be.

BIBLE STUDY   Ephesians 2:4-7

WARM-UP   Did you ever wonder…

✓ Why people recite at a play and play at a recital?

✓ How a slim chance and a fat chance can be the same thing?

✓ Why you fill in a form by filling it out?

PERSONAL STUDY   When pondering life's deeper mysteries, do you instinctively turn for insight to…your local sportscaster? If not, I guess maybe you don't live in Philadelphia.

The sports radio talk-show hosts in this city are amazing. History, stats, the sports rumor-mill—they know it all. These guys have clearly devoted their lives to gathering every conceivable fact about sports, and their listeners love it. It's during those rare lulls in sports activity, however, that faithful listeners experience the flip side of such exquisite specialization. As the sportscasters are forced to venture into non-sports talk, we quickly learn that these guys don't have the first clue about anything *except* sports!

One desperate time-filler that runs during these lulls is called the "Mystery Question of Life." In this segment, poor, bewildered callers submit their "Mystery Questions" to these philosopher wanna-bes. Do you lie awake at night wondering why there are roughing penalties in full-contact sports? Or why we drive on parkways and park on driveways? These are the kinds of deep issues tackled on slow sports days in my town.

What is your Mystery Question of Life? It's probably

something a little more weighty than the ones mentioned above. Maybe it's, "Lord, why did you make me the way I am?", "Why did you allow this to happen to me?", or "Will my life ever amount to anything?" Mystery Questions are the ones that linger at the edge of thought, unanswered and unwanted, ready to move in and rudely rearrange one's emotional furniture at the slightest invitation.

These "Who am I?" and "Where am I going?" questions are universal. At one time or another, we all ask them: when reflecting on the difficulties or failures of our past; when honestly examining the gaps between who we are and who we project ourselves to be; or when pondering the uncertainties of the future and the potential implications of our decisions. They are unsettling questions because they can upset our most comfortable assumptions about ourselves.

I, Me, Mine: Single in the Culture of Self

Few people are paralyzed by these "Who am I?" questions, but all of us live with their influence on a daily basis. Christians are no different in this regard—how we deal with them determines our decisions and our general outlook on life. As a single adult you no doubt have your own take on the "Who am I?" problem.

The current secular solution is to focus on "self-hood," as if how I feel about myself is the key to identity. Here is the secular mindset: we are fragile, innocent, and frequently victimized creatures who need to continually cultivate love of self. My selfhood has been shaped by what others did (or didn't) do to me (or for me) in the past. A pleasant past produces a generally "healthy" sense of self. A difficult past produces "inadequacies." My goal is to "know myself," to "make peace with myself," and to "like myself." My future selfhood depends on how well I protect myself from those who would harm me. The ultimate goal of this secular mindset is to love ourselves as fully as possible. Self-love becomes the cornerstone of a "healthy" and

> **"** As our culture shouts loud messages to us about who we're supposed to be and what we're supposed to do to be fulfilled, growing numbers of Christians are becoming confused about their identity and purpose....When we inadequately exalt God and instead exalt ourselves openly or subtly, aware or unaware, then we make ourselves vulnerable to wrong perceptions about ourselves.[1] **"**
>
> — Carol Cornish

"well-adjusted" sense of personhood. It is the proposed secular solution to our Mystery Questions of Life.

A multimillion-dollar industry has grown up around this preoccupation with, as one critic calls it, the "Imperial Self." Much of the information directed to the Christian single adult demonstrates the impact of this Culture of Self on the church. Consider the following quote from a popular book for Christian singles:

> Singlehood is a state of existence, a way of being. It is a condition of encouraging, affirming, and maintaining one's integrity as a *self*. It is being willing—and learning how—to become increasingly *self-aware, self-preserving, self-affirming, self-fulfilling*, and autonomous *(self-governing)*.[2] [italics supplied]

Meditate on Philippians 2:5-11.
How would Jesus' approach to his purpose differ from what we are often told about how we should view ourselves?

---

1 Which of the following terms reflect a biblical understanding of human problems?

❏ Bitterness   ❏ Insecurity   ❏ Anxiety

❏ Depression   ❏ Laziness   ❏ Selfishness

❏ Frustration   ❏ Shame   ❏ Jealousy

❏ Moodiness

Or consider this advice from a handbook for pastors of single adults:

> The church has a role in helping the single adult to become aware and accepting of *self*. The goal is to become overcomers of low *self-image*...the church can assist the single in learning how to make a *self-commitment*. Whether individual or group counseling, the result of the work must be found in the principle for *self-esteem*.[3] [italics supplied]

The problem with Christians adopting this self-centered approach to identity is that it teaches the exact opposite of Scripture, so it can never please God or lead us to him for help. In contrast to the secular approach, biblical truth on self can be summed up in two points:

1. One thing we *don't* lack is love for ourselves. (Mt 19:19, 2Ti 3:2)

2. Far from being fragile and innocent, our selves are rebellious and willful. (Ro 7:25, 12:3)

God does not portray himself in Scripture as a facilitator of our self-image goals. Rather, he is the one to whom we must give account for every selfish, sinful word and deed. A Christian single who embraces the Culture of Self is missing out. The world has promised you answers that are nothing but worthless counterfeits.

A preoccupation with Self drives us to view everything and everyone crossing our path as having meaning primarily based on the way they affect us right now. Relationships become self-serving. Possessions become our security. Our thanksgiving and worship toward God are driven by our assessment of how well he does what we want him to do (we call it "meeting our needs"). The Christian immersed in the Culture of Self is preoccupied with the temporal, while the eternal lies unappreciated and unexplored. To be trapped in Self is to lack both the joy of living in the good of God's love, and the only effective means of wrestling with the daily questions of life.

For Further Study:
Read 2 Timothy 3:1-5. What kinds of love will people have who possess a form of godliness but deny its power?

> **❝** It is not the obliteration of personal identity to which the gospel calls us but to the realization that our worth and merit before God come to us from outside, not from within, as a gift, a charitable donation.[4] **❞**
>
> — **Don Matzat**

If the search for meaning and order cannot be found in the love of self, where do we look? Why not go back to where your new life began?

2 The particular facts a Christian emphasizes when sharing the gospel message often say a lot about how he or she views God. Which of the following was most prominent in the message you heard when you gave your life to Christ?

❏ Only God can straighten out your messed-up life

❏ You are in a free fall toward Hell without a parachute

❏ God loves you and has a wonderful plan for your life

❏ Jesus is just, like, so totally incredibly awesome

❏ Christianity is the only true way to know God

❏ Other:

Living in the Good of the Gospel

I often think back to my salvation experience, the serene peace of the days that followed, and the wonder of having been freed from a rebellious lifestyle. But I also remember my first major post-conversion eruption of selfish pride. I was a Christian now, I wasn't supposed to be prideful! Suddenly I felt I was teetering on the brink of spiritual chaos. Seeing more sin in my life than ever before, I wrote in my journal, "How many times and in how many ways do I willingly turn my eyes from You, Lord. Discouragement is knocking at my door. My eyes have been turned on myself. There are so many needs around and all I see are my own problems." I felt like God's first failure.

About that time someone suggested I memorize Romans Chapter 6. I was desperate—desperate enough to memorize Scripture. As I ran the verses through my mind during the next few weeks, some very helpful truth started to seep in. I began to realize that the gospel is not just about rescue from trouble. It's about taking on a new identity (vv. 1-8). I saw that, prior to my conversion, I had not been just an independent person who happened to be a sinner. Like every other non-Christian, I was *enslaved* by sin. Sin had owned me with an ironclad deed. In receiving Christ I was not simply being forgiven, I was being bought by a new owner. I was now a "slave to God" (v. 22). The "free gift" of God (v. 23) was actually his ownership of my life.

> **"** Who am I, Lord, to know You? What have I, oh Lord, to show You? Just the grateful heart of a sinner who loves grace.[5] **"**
>
> — **Mark Altrogge**

It was then that I finally began to understand God's grace. Grace wasn't manifested simply in God's mercy for my abundant failures (as wonderful as that is), but also in a desire and an ability within me to live in "grateful slavery" to God. I saw that the central issue in the Christian's life is no longer "Who am I?", but "Whose I am." This realization brought a security that has remained with me for more than 15 years.

Yet God's purchase of us did not come cheaply. It cost the life of his dear, innocent Son, Jesus. The Cross of Christ establishes God's right of ownership over his people. That ownership has as its goal *relationship*—worshipful and reverent, yes, but intimate and secure as well: relationship to the glory of God. The amazing truth of the Cross is that the God who had supreme rights to punish rebellious sinners,

Meditate on Romans 6:20-23. Can you think of any real benefits of being free from the control of righteousness? What is the result of this "freedom"?

> **"** The fellowship of God is delightful beyond all telling. He communes with His redeemed ones in an easy, uninhibited fellowship that is restful and healing to the soul. He is not sensitive nor selfish nor temperamental. What He is today we shall find Him tomorrow and the next day and the next year. He is not hard to please, though He may be hard to satisfy. He expects of us only what He has Himself first supplied. He is quick to mark every simple effort to please Him, and just as quick to overlook imperfections when He knows we meant to do His will. He loves us for ourselves and values our love more than galaxies of new created worlds.[6] **"**
>
> — **A.W. Tozer**

instead chose freely to die for them (us). His death did not merely purchase our freedom from the tyranny of sin, it placed us under God's care and in God's family. This is good news. This is the gospel of peace.

As the Apostle Paul tells it:

> When the time had fully come, God sent his Son, born of a woman, born under law, to redeem those under law, that we might receive the full rights of sons. Because you are sons, God sent the Spirit of his Son into our hearts, the Spirit who calls out, "Abba, Father." So you are no longer a slave, but a son; and since you are a son, God has made you also an heir (Gal 4:4-7).

Let's look at what this amazingly good news means for us in all seasons—how the Cross answers the most profound Mystery Questions of Life: past, present, and future.

Your Past in the Shadow of the Cross

One thing the Culture of Self gets right is this: We all have events in our past that shape our lives. It's in interpreting and dealing with these events that the secular approach goes hopelessly off course.

What event has most shaped who you are? Ask this question in a church small-group study and you are liable to get a universal response: The day I became a Christian. But if you asked the same people in private, or if you were to follow them around and observe their lives (not recommended!) you might well arrive at a very different answer. While every Christian's actual most important event was the day he or she received Christ, for many the *functional* most important event might be altogether different.

Maybe it was the day when those cherished hopes of making the high school football team were smashed, or the day the family dog died. Maybe it was when the sexual

For Further Study:
Read Colossians 2:13-15. Make a list of all the action verbs used in this passage to describe the power of the Cross.

molestation began. Or it could be something far less traumatic—one person's most important event might seem trivial to someone else.

Before I became a Christian, I was in a run of relationships where I was the "dumpee" (that is, *she* broke up with *me*). After I was married, I counted the occasions. The total was something like 18 dumpings before my high school graduation, compared to only one time when I chose to end a relationship. That's a .056 batting average! Maybe I was overshooting my social limits. Maybe I was just a dweeb. Probably both. In any event, that has to be some kind of record. It sure felt like one, and over time this abysmal streak of dumpings contributed to suspicious and manipulative tendencies in my relationships with women. Other things have happened to me that you might consider far more devastating, but for years nothing affected me more in my day-to-day life than that pitiful .056.

> **"** Every harsh word spoken;
> every promise ever broken to me
> Total recall, of data in the memory
> Every tear that has washed my face;
> every moment of disgrace that I have known
> Every time I've ever felt alone
> Lord of the here and now;
> Lord of the come what may
> I want to believe somehow
> that you can heal these wounds of yesterday
> So now I'm asking you,
> to do what you want to do
> Be the Lord of the past.[7] **"**
> — **Bob Bennett**

---

3 Your life story has been made into a movie. Which of the following advertisement lines would most accurately describe this production:

❏ "A sweeping spectacle"   ❏ "A dark comedy"

❏ "An edge-of-the-seat thriller"   ❏ "A moving saga"

❏ "A slapstick hoot"   ❏ (other)_____

We all have experiences that have written themselves into our lives. Everybody has a story, and that story has enormous implications for who we are and where we are going. As counselor John Bettler describes it, "Sometimes your story looks like science fiction. Sometimes your story looks like fantasy. Sometimes your story looks like tragedy. Sometimes it's a comedy. But your story is a story, and your story is yours."[8]

For Further Study:
Read Psalm 107. List
the problems the peo-
ple had that were not
their fault. List the
problems the people
had that they brought
on themselves. Is there
any difference in God's
response to their cries?

Dr. Bettler goes on to note that our memory of events is "active, selective, and creative." When it comes to the stories of our lives, we are not just camera operators, we are directors, scriptwriters, editors, and actors. We determine which scenes to keep and which to cut, how much weight to give to various plot lines, and what emotional score should fill in the background. No one can tell our story like we can! Based on my own experience and that of people I have counseled, here are a few other helpful observations about what gets written into our personal stories.

Your perception of who you are tends to be shaped by things that are negative. If you could list the ten most vivid memories of your life, how many would be positive? How many negative? For me, all the many wonderful moments from my past kind of blend together as "good times." My sharpest memories tend to be of unpleasant things. It's like the movies. If you watch a good comedy, you might recall some funny moments. But a frightening film can leave mental images that echo in your mind with alarming power for days and weeks to come. If left to write your own script, you will tend to write it as a tragedy.

Your perception of who you are tends to be shaped by what happened to you, not by what you did. In college I was on the soccer team. When I began to feel the coach was out to get me, I did the only thing I knew to do. I quit in a huff, a martyr to the cause of Me. As far as I was concerned, that coach had ruined my promising career. When he left before the next school year began, I returned to the team, my righteous stance against unjust persecution vindicated.

Years later it hit me: the coach had only treated me as my behavior deserved. I was a slacker! I didn't deserve even to be on the field. Yet for years I held a bitter attitude toward that man. If not for God graciously showing me how I squandered my soccer opportunity because of pride, I would still be bitter today. There were two sides to that story. Mine was wrong.

A negative view of your past is often based on some perception of a "normal" experience that you were "denied." One of the leading Culture of Self buzzwords is "dysfunctional." The theory of the "dysfunctional" family assumes there is such a thing as a fully functional family, and that every human being possesses some inalienable right to have had one. Have you ever met a normal family? I haven't—and that includes the one I'm raising.

For Further Study:
Read the story of
Joseph in Genesis 37
and 39-47. What raw
deals did Joseph have
to endure that could
have made him bitter?

That's because original sin has "dysfunctionalized" every relationship.

While the label "dysfunctional" is gradually receding into the waste bin of overripe fads, we still tend to think along these lines (people always have and always will), because sin drives us continually to feel sorry for ourselves. We tend to include in our personal definition of a "normal" life precisely those things we didn't get. A father who expressed biblical love; parents who stayed together; being accepted for who you are—statistics and experience show that such "normal" expectations are more the exception than the rule. Still, our sin nature insists we have somehow been cheated. In the final analysis, we are blaming God for messing up our lives.

Your outlook on life is often held hostage by decisions you made long ago. Suppose you're sitting in a park one day and a five-year-old comes up to you and says, "The secret to life is to do whatever you can to get what you want." A few minutes later a twelve-year-old comes up and mutters, "The most important thing in life is that everyone likes you." Finally a 16-year-old walks over and proclaims, "Independence and rebellion are the only things that really bring happiness." Would you decide then and there to structure your life around any one of these dubious insights? Not hardly. Yet have you ever stopped to think how much of your life today is shaped by decisions you made and opinions you formed when you were young? You were bitten by a dog and now are fearful of animals. You were called "tubby" in grade school and now the most important discipline you have is physical fitness. These immature pacts we make with ourselves often have great sway over the course of our lives.

---

4 Are there any views of life that you hold right now, that you suspect may be wrong or exaggerated, and that you probably formed when you were a child? In the space below, write the first such view that comes to mind.

In his second letter to the Corinthian church, the Apostle Paul wrote:

And he died for all, that those who live should no longer live for themselves but for him who died for them and was raised again. So from now on we regard no one from a worldly point of view. Though we once regarded Christ in this way, we do so no longer. Therefore, if anyone is in Christ, he is a new creation; the old has gone, the new has come! (2Co 5:15-17)

The atoning work of Christ on the Cross is the line of demarcation between our limiting past and our future of promise. For all who have received the new birth, the Cross becomes the most important event in our lives. God is "on the set" and he is reworking the drama of our past with a new ending and a new theme. Rather than a tragedy of despair and loss, our past becomes the telling of an adventure—sometimes frightening, sometimes thrilling, often with mystery, but always with purpose.

And the Cross does more. In the forgiveness of God, the Cross provides the remedy for the shame of our sin. Less often noted is the fact that the Cross also speaks to our unjust sufferings. For many, the most profound aspect of our lives is our suffering. The Cross recognizes our unjust suffering, for in his death Jesus endured the most horrible and unjust suffering in history. Of the crucifixion, Isaiah writes with prophetic horror:

> He was oppressed and afflicted, yet he did not open his mouth; he was led like a lamb to the slaughter, and as a sheep before her shearers is silent, so he did not open his mouth. By oppression and judgment he was taken away. And who can speak of his descendants? For he was cut off from the land of the living; for the transgression of my people he was stricken. He was assigned a grave with the wicked, and with the rich in his death, though he had done no violence, nor was any deceit in his mouth. Yet it was the LORD's will to crush him and cause him to suffer (Isa 53:7-10).

Does Jesus say, "My suffering was worse than you'll

Meditate on 1 Corinthians 1:18. How have you seen the power of the Cross at work in your life?

> The cross proclaims power to the weak, a lifting up for the humbled, a covering for the naked, love for those who have been hated, redemption for those who are slaves, grace for those who are trying to pay for their sins, forgiveness for sinners, and judgement on the enemies of God.[9]
>
> **— Ed Welch**

ever know, so stop whining!"? No. "The Lord is full of compassion and mercy" (Jas 5:11). His suffering was for our benefit, and he promises he will never leave or forsake us. Through the Cross we come to better understand justice and mercy; we see the possibility of glorifying God in our suffering; we grasp the meaning behind the phrase "entering into the fellowship of sharing in his sufferings" (Php 3:10); we experience his joy and "peace that surpasses all comprehension" (Php 4:7, NAS); life takes on an eternal perspective; and we become able to truly forgive all our oppressors. These realities may be as shadows in the mist to you right now, but God is at work bringing them into full view in your life.

Meditate on Psalm 22:1-18. Take a few moments to contemplate the physical anguish Jesus endured because of your sin.

A man in our church, whose father was continually in and out of mental institutions, lived for years with bitterness toward God for the difficulties in his life associated with his father's condition. Gradually, he began to see his suffering in light of God's glory. A breakthrough came when God spoke to his heart sovereignly as he listened to a sermon on heaven. As he describes it, "I think the glory of Christ began to break in on my heart. Slowly but surely God revealed my pride and arrogance in thinking that the God of the universe owed me explanations for the circumstances in my life. I wept with appreciation for God's incredible mercy and patience with me. It dawned on me that though my circumstances had produced great personal pain, they also had been hand-selected by a loving and all-knowing God to produce good things in my life that only they could produce. God graciously allowed me to experience several months of fellowship and reconciliation with my father before he passed away. I look forward to experiencing fellowship now with my heavenly Father without me placing demands on him to make sense of my life."

In a Culture of Self where the problems of the past continually invade the present, the Cross of Christ in the gospel of Christ is at work invading our past—overturning lies, redefining events, and extending the light of the glory of God into the darkest memories of our lives.

Your Present: Living in View of the Cross

If the Cross has purchased us from sin and redefined our past, it also has meaning in the present. What are some implications of the Cross in our daily lives?

Living on the altar. In Romans 12:1, Paul writes, "Therefore, I urge you, brothers, in view of God's mercy,

ACCOUNTABILITY AND THE SINGLE CHRISTIAN

We often talk about the need for accountability in order to grow consistently in the Christian life. What is accountability? Is it having someone I can share my struggles with? Someone who will tell me things I need to do to grow? Do I always have to be in an accountability relationship?

Here are some tips based on my personal perspective on accountability and how it can work in your life.

1. We are, first and last, accountable to God. He is the only one we need to please.
2. Accountability requires trust, but doesn't necessarily require a close personal relationship to be effective.
3. Accountability can be formal, like a group of guys getting together on a weekly basis to share and pray. Or it can be informal, like two friends who know each other well enough to ask the right questions.
4. Accountability may not necessarily require anyone to exercise authority over another person. Accountability is not counseling. It is simply holding up God's standard to someone who has expressed a desire to be reminded of it.
5. Accountability is the responsibility of the person seeking it. In other words, if I come to you and ask you to hold me accountable in an area of my life, you shouldn't have to seek me out to find out how I'm doing. I should be actively pursuing you to keep you up to date on how I'm doing.

Here are some questions, adapted from various sources, that have been proven to help develop good accountability.

1. How consistent have you been in your spiritual disciplines during the past month?
2. Have you related to anyone during the past month in a way that would not reflect respect, biblical love, and sexual and moral purity?
3. Have you expressed any attitudes or actions in your work environment during the past month that would negatively reflect on your testimony for Christ?
4. Are you experiencing any unreconciled relationships?
5. Has your giving or any of your financial dealings lacked integrity or wisdom?
6. Are any of the following sins a particular struggle for you right now: Moral Impurity, Slothfulness, Complaining, Jealousy, or Gossip.
7. Would your friends say that you are open to correction or input right now?
8. (Men) Have you allowed yourself to be involved with any sexually explicit material during the past month?
(Women) Have you expressed any tendency which could indicate too much concern for your appearance during the past month?

to offer your bodies as living sacrifices, holy and pleasing to God—this is your spiritual act of worship." Paul is talking here about consecration (setting ourselves apart), not for religion, but for spiritual purpose and growth. Being living sacrifices means establishing personal convictions rooted in biblical truth, and living under them, even when they produce hardship. It means embracing the discipline and conviction of God as good things, not as hindrances to life as I would prefer to live it. Living on the altar means welcoming the weight of the Cross into your life every day.

The problem with being living sacrifices is that we have this annoying habit of continually crawling down off the altar. If life on the altar doesn't flow with the ordinary current of this world (and it doesn't), why embrace it? Paul's answer is inspiring: "Do not conform any longer to the pattern of this world, but be transformed by the renewing of your mind. Then you will be able to test and approve what God's will is—his good, pleasing and perfect will" (Ro 12:2).

For Further Study:
Read Hebrews 10:19–25. Why can we offer ourselves to God with joyful confidence?

The gospel holds out the promise of a transformed life, a life lived above the ordinary. To experience this life we must dedicate ourselves to the pursuit of it—through grace-motivated obedience to God's good, pleasing, and perfect will. If you desire to experience this transformed life, maybe it's time to crawl up on the altar and get a better view. That is devotion, our spiritual act of worship.

Fleeing me. Before I became a Christian, temptation wasn't a problem—usually it was thrilling! But with salvation comes an awareness that temptation never leads us anywhere good. Suddenly, temptation becomes a battle. But what exactly do we battle against?

> ❝ Your worst days are never so bad that you are beyond the *reach* of God's grace. And your best days are never so good that you are beyond the *need* of God's grace.[10] ❞
>
> — **Jerry Bridges**

One of the traps Christians can fall into is the avoidance of understanding temptation. Not the avoidance of temptation (which is obviously important), but of *understanding temptation*. The reasoning goes something like this: "Why should I think about temptation and just make it worse?" But the biblical approach to temptation is to see it clearly as the serious threat to our growth that it is. Throughout Scripture, the temptations of God's people are displayed in all their ugliness. Even Jesus is described as being tempted (Lk 4:2), which illustrates an important truth: temptation itself is not sin. But where there is temptation, the potential for sin is very near, so an awareness of the nature and remedy for temptation is vital.

Here are some other important realities about temptation. God never tempts us (Jas 1:13). We can, however, be tempted by our own desires (Jas 1:14); by the carnal world (1Jn 2:15-17); and by Satan (1Co 7:5). There are NO temptations so extraordinary or captivating that we cannot resist with God's ready help (1Co 10:12-13).

Possibly the most important thing to know, however, is this: our struggle with temptation is actually *evidence of God's grace in our lives*. Back in my old memory passage, Romans 6, Paul explains that when we were slaves to sin we were free from righteousness; that is, we had no reason to respond to anything but temptation. Now we are slaves of righteousness, and temptation matters to us, because it doesn't fit into God's ownership plan for our lives.

Meditate on James 1:12-15. Why is it important not to flirt with temptation?

---

5 Which of the following temptations would you find most enticing?

❏ A rich, well-made chocolate dessert

❏ An undisturbed nap on a Sunday afternoon

❏ Command of the remote control, 120 channels to surf, and six hours of free time, alone

❏ A Mall-wide 50%-Off sale

Can you imagine circumstances in which yielding to some of these temptations would be sinful for you? Are there other circumstances in which it would not be sin?

So what do we do with temptation? First, in facing it, don't be surprised at what you see. The doctrine of indwelling sin tells us that, although the *dominion* of sin over our lives has been broken, the *activity* of sin remains. We are by nature lustful, rebellious, and foolish creatures who operate 24-hour-a-day, 7-day-a-week idol factories in our hearts. Nothing should surprise us. Yet the good news is that we have been rescued and are being changed into ever-greater likenesses of our Rescuer, Jesus Christ. We need not be carried away by temptation, but we must be watchful for its attempts to grab us. And the better we understand temptation, the more watchful we can be.

For Further Study:
Read Luke 4:1-13. What did Jesus use to resist the temptations of the Devil? Is there anything he did in this encounter that we cannot do?

Second, recognize that the Bible has one principal defense against temptation: FLEE! (1Co 6:18, 10:14; 1Ti 6:11; 2Ti 2:22) What does it mean to flee? Consider…roaches.

As soon as a roach knows trouble is near he starts running. Where he goes doesn't really matter, he just *goes*. That's kind of what fleeing should be for us. Next time you chase a roach around the kitchen, stop a moment and take notes on his fleeing techniques. They could come in handy. (OK, I know there are some exceptionally arrogant and/or stupid roaches that flee less readily, but look what happens to them!)

And did you ever notice that God tells us to resist Satan but flee from temptation? *This means that little old you and me will have a lot more success fighting against the prince of darkness than against our own sinful desires!* In fact, James 4:7 says that if we resist (battle) the devil *he* will actually do the roach scamper from *us*.

Finally, remember that Jesus himself is ready to help us out of temptation. "Because he himself suffered when he was tempted, he is able to help those who are being tempted" (Heb 2:18). And if we do sin after being tempted, God provides a way back through confession, repentance, and faith (1Jn 1:9). God's ability to help us in time of need and restore us in time of fall is an essential part of our growth under his loving ownership.

Meditate on 1 Corinthians 10:13.
How can it be helpful in times of temptation to know that God won't allow you to be tempted beyond what you can bear?

Walking by the Spirit. Puritan pastor/theologian John Owen had a wonderful description of the work of Holy Spirit. He called the Spirit "the beautifier of souls."[12]

In the divine ownership plan, the Holy Spirit is the master craftsman, the foreman of God's renovation work in our lives. He carries out his job in a number of ways. He makes sure God's work goes according to specifications ("guides us into all truth," Jn 16:13-15); shores up weak spots (Ro 8:26); gives us unique features and functions (1Co 12:4-11); and stamps "PROPERTY OF GOD" all over us ("The Spirit himself testifies with our spirit that we are God's children," Ro 8:16).

But we're not just piles of building material waiting for the Craftsman to start hammering away. God's ownership means we can take part in the construction. Gordon Fee writes, "Life in the Spirit is not passive submission to the Spirit to do a supernatural work in one's life; rather, it requires conscious effort, so that the indwelling Spirit may accomplish His ends in one's life."[13] This cooperative effort is what Paul is talking about when he exhorts those who "belong to Christ" to "keep in step with the Spirit" (Gal 5:24-25). While the Holy Spirit/Master Craftsman is doing the work of beautification in us, we are the laborers whose effort is somehow important to the project. Jerry Bridges puts it this way: "God's work does not make our effort unnecessary, but rather makes it effective."[14]

> 66 God is at work creating eternal changes at the level of my heart, in my true desires and hopes. He is drawing me away from hope in this present world to hope in Him alone. He is revealing true life to me, life that consists of the all-surpassing power of Christ Jesus living within me. And He will use the things of this present world—often the loss of them—to accomplish this grand redemptive agenda. His goal is not the abundance of earthly things, but the abundance of hope in God.[15] 99
>
> — **Paul Tripp**

The Future: Living Today in the Light of Eternity

Thus far in this study we have discussed how the Cross provides overcoming power for our past and constructive power in our present. But how does the Cross shape our future? It is this question that will occupy much of the rest of this book.

For the Christian, the future begins at this moment and extends to eternity. We therefore will look at our goals, choices, and opportunities as single adults in light of the Cross. It is here that the words of Jesus provide both marching orders and assurance of victory for the future: "If anyone would come after me, he must deny himself and take up his cross daily and follow me. For whoever wants to save his life will lose it, but whoever loses his life for me will save it" (Lk 9:23-24).

For the Christian, the "Who am I?" questions must be answered both negatively (rejecting the lies of the world) and positively (embracing the truth of Scripture).

Who I am not:

• I am not the sum total of my self-perceptions.

• I am not the accumulated facts of my life history.

• I am not what others believe about me.

***Whose* I am not:**

• I am not my own; I do not belong to myself. (Ro 14:8, 1 Co 6:19-20)

Whose I am:

• I am God's child, bought with an incalculable price, set apart for noble purposes. (1Jn 3:1, Ac 20:28)

• I am God's workmanship, and he who began a good work in me will be faithful to complete it. (Eph 2:10, Php 1:6)

May these words, taken from a song written by my friend Chris Wright, reflect your ambitions for the rich single life.

There's a cross on a hill—can you see it?
The price He freely paid
Lifted up for you
Lifted up, it's for you

It's for you He came
It's for you He suffered
And He died, His Father's will to do
If we choose to follow Him
Our lives we must deny...

There's a cross in the road, can you see it?
A choice that must be made
Lift it up...it's for you
Pick it up...it's for you[16] ∎

GROUP DISCUSSION 1. What types of situations tend to make you think about the deeper questions of life?

2. How has the secular understanding of self-hood influenced you?

3. At what point after you were saved did you realize that the battle with temptation and sin was part of the Christian life?

4. What is the greatest difference between God's father-

hood as revealed in Scripture and your experience with your earthly father?

5. Describe a time in your childhood when you were aware that God existed and cared for you.

6. In what ways has your relationship with God helped you understand things from your past?

7. What methods of fleeing temptation have you found to be most effective?

8. How have you seen the Holy Spirit at work in your life?

9. What does it mean to take up your cross at this time in your life?

RECOMMENDED READING

The Discipline of Grace by Jerry Bridges (Colorado Springs, CO: NavPress, 1994)

When People Are Big and God is Small by Edward T. Welch (Phillipsburg, NJ: Presbyterian and Reformed, 1997)

Women Helping Women edited by Elyse Fitzpatrick and Carol Cornish (Eugene, OR: Harvest House Publishers, 1997)

RICH IN VISION

Strategy: The rich single life mines the essence of our identity and season of life for the hidden treasures of opportunity.

BIBLE STUDY   1 Peter 1:10-11

WARM-UP   How well do you know the recent history of the sexual revolution? Draw lines to match these important events with the year in which they occurred.

National Organization of Women begins •   • **1982**

Billie Jean King beats Bobby Riggs
in the Battle of the Sexes (Tennis Version) •   • **1997**

Susan B. Anthony Dollar introduced •   • **1966**

Ms. Pac-Man becomes more popular as a
video game than Pac-Man •   • **1979**

Ellen DeGeneres: The closet episode •   • **1973**

(See page 51 for answers)

PERSONAL STUDY   The classroom was stuffed with small huddles of posturing undergrads as I walked through the door on that first day of my junior year. It was a large group, especially for an upper-level college elective course. As I scanned the room, I recognized most of my fellow political-science majors. There was also a healthy sampling of frat guys, balanced by an equal number of outspoken feminists. Sprinkled in among them were some fine-arts punks, science brains, and aspiring intellectuals. This had the makings of a most entertaining semester.

Only a course entitled "The Politics of Sex" could have brought us all together that day. I won't speculate on the motivations of my fellow students, but my reasons for being there were not exclusively academic. To my dismay, however, I soon discovered that the course content would

> **❝** As I worked with a wide variety of women, I began to notice something. It was clear that many of the women I talked to had been seriously mistreated. Some of them had faced great injustice in their lives. It was hardly surprising that they felt angry and bitter. Certainly, it was important to seek justice for them. Yet I noticed that these women had a problem whose roots went far deeper than discrimination. Even if they were given justice, they would still be left with the problem of their own anger and resentment, with their dissatisfaction with life.[1] **❞**
>
> — Dee Jepsen

be less about sex and more about politics. "Gender and the Struggle for Equality" would have been a more accurate course title, but far less attractive on sign-up day.

The premise of the course was that all of life is a political struggle for power, rights, and freedoms, and nowhere is this struggle more aggressively played out than in the relationships between men and women. As if to demonstrate this premise, the class soon broke into two camps—the traditionalists (mostly male), and the progressives (mostly female). The rest of the semester was basically one big battle of the sexes, producing heavy ego casualties on both sides. I don't recall the entire class ever agreeing on anything, except maybe where to have the keg party at the end of the term.

---

1 We all have times where we stumble onto the battlefield in the war between the sexes. Maybe you're a woman who waits for a man to open the door and it shuts in your face. Maybe you are a man who has been challenged on a politically incorrect term in conversation. In your last foray into the battle of the sexes, which of the following would best describe the experience?

❑ A tug of war   ❑ A cold war

❑ An ambush   ❑ Guerrilla warfare

For Further Study:
Read Genesis 3. What was the woman's contribution to the fall into sin? What was the man's contribution?

In splitting into two camps, the class reflected our society's schism over the "Sexual Revolution," that disastrous experiment begun in the 1960s. Regardless of gender or political beliefs, you and I are participants in this ongoing experiment. It's an experiment because it involves tampering with society's view of sex and how we see each other as sexual beings. It is a revolution because nearly every sphere of life—morality, law, entertainment, customs, economics—has been shaken and shaped by it. Decades after it began, this revolution remains a topic of heated debate. In the minds of some, it is destroying the very foundations of society. Others see any remaining obstacles to complete sexual license as repression of the cruelest kind. Meanwhile, revolution continues to swirl all around us.

Sexual Politics and the Church

Meditate on Proverbs 26:17. Have you ever stumbled into a debate and regretted it? How should you approach these situations?

Don't look now, but the sexual revolution is alive and kicking in the church as well. Some of the most divisive issues in the church today, such as the debate over women in ministry and the idea of a gender-neutral Bible, are a direct result of the encroachment of sexual politics into the Christian culture. Although most biblical scholarship affirms the traditional understanding of male/female roles and identities, the debates rage on. Often, opposing sides can't even agree on the question, much less the answer. Is the church stuck in outmoded and legalistic ways of thinking? Or are Scripture and Christian tradition being abandoned for a liberal political agenda that exalts human desires above God's law?

In these debates, liberals tend to envision a culture that emphasizes human freedom and equality as the highest possible good. Such a culture, however, could never bring human satisfaction, for the simple reason that it rejects God's laws regarding moral behavior for mankind.

Meanwhile, conservatives tend to look to the past for inspiration. Conservative Christians can appeal to almost any pre-1960 period of cultural history, as long as it was "more Christian" than our own. But we would do far better to take our life cues from the infallible Scripture rather than from the traditions of our all-too-fallible predecessors.

A humble study of the Bible and history reveals that those long-lost "good old days" prior to the sexual revolution were hardly a heaven-on-earth. Grievous injustice toward women, in plain violation of Scripture, has regularly been tolerated throughout Christian history, simply because then-current secular culture and traditions found it acceptable. In fact, some notable Christian thinkers believe the sexual revolution was ushered in by the failure of twentieth-century men and women to rightly exercise their biblical roles and responsibilities.

The practical result has been great confusion—some-

For Further Study: Read James 5:13. What will help us keep from evaluating others on the basis of our own limited cultural understandings?

35

times even within the church—over what it means to be a man, what it means to be a woman, and how the two can possibly co-exist. How can you express your unique attributes as a man or woman under Christ in this gender-blended culture? How can you confidently stand against the cultural tide without becoming entangled in the political push-and-shove that so often characterizes this debate? Space doesn't permit me to set out an apologetic against a feminist view of the biblical treatment of women; the recommended reading at the end of this study can help you there. But I do believe that the rhetoric of the sexual revolution can do great harm within the church, primarily by muddling our understanding of the wonderful and complementary purpose of gender identities presented in Scripture.

> **“** Apart from a widespread national return to God, never again will the followers of Christ be able to take their sexual cues from this society. We must fend for ourselves, forge out our own biblical ethic, and enforce it where we can. In the process we must open wide our doors and invite in those weary pilgrims made open to Christian faith because they have tasted the bitter waters of the world's sorry alternative.[2] **”**
>
> — **Randy Alcorn**

Early on in writing this book I realized I would, at some point, have to address single men and women separately, for men and women approach the life of faith in very different ways. My problem, obviously, is that I only see through male eyes. I have tried to compensate by studying and seeking help from the women I know, especially my extraordinary wife, Jill, who has coached me for 14 years. So here's my shot at this task. I hope you find it helpful.

Single Women: Keep the Flame

In Matthew 25, Jesus shares parables on how to prepare for the coming of the Kingdom of God. One parable concerns ten maidens who are waiting for the arrival of a bridegroom:

> At that time the kingdom of heaven will be like ten virgins who took their lamps and went out to meet the bridegroom. Five of them were foolish and five were wise. The foolish ones took their lamps but did not take any oil with them. The wise, however, took oil in jars along with their lamps. The bridegroom was a long time in coming, and they all became

drowsy and fell asleep. At midnight the cry rang out: "Here's the bridegroom! Come out to meet him!" Then all the virgins woke up and trimmed their lamps. The foolish ones said to the wise, "Give us some of your oil; our lamps are going out." "No," they replied, "there may not be enough for both us and you. Instead, go to those who sell oil and buy some for yourselves." But while they were on their way to buy the oil, the bridegroom arrived. The virgins who were ready went in with him to the wedding banquet. And the door was shut. Later the others also came. "Sir! Sir!" they said. "Open the door for us!" But he replied, "I tell you the truth, I don't know you." Therefore keep watch, because you do not know the day or the hour (Mt 25:1-13).

Meditate on Luke 21:34-36. In what ways might you lack readiness for Christ's return?

This parable is clearly about the need for every person to be wise in preparation because we don't know when Christ will return. Jesus uses a culturally familiar scene of ten maidens (the Greek word used here is *parthenos*, meaning "mature young women") who are performing the traditional duty of lighting the way of the bridegroom. Their "lamps" were probably torches on long poles with wicks that needed to be soaked in a flammable oil to remain lit.

If you were a "parthenos" listening to Jesus tell this parable, you might find yourself quite concerned about the choices made by the five foolish single women. Their lack of readiness cost them dearly. No doubt the first thing you would do when you got home that night would be to check your own oil supply!

For the Christian single woman, today's messages about the requirements of femininity pose dizzying contradictions. Take a look at any magazine stand. What is the most important thing a woman needs? Independence? The right man? Equality in the workplace? Great nails? Proponents of the sexual revolution claim that women have always lacked independent identity, that they have been defined primarily in relation to men.

> ❝ At the heart of mature femininity is a freeing disposition to affirm, receive and nurture strength and leadership from worthy men in ways appropriate to a woman's differing relationships.[3] ❞
>
> — **John Piper**

Feminist leader Patricia Ireland writes, "The essence of feminism for me is the freedom to live our lives as we please, and to reinvent the world as we do so."[4] Helen

> **❝** I'm tough, ambitious, and I know exactly what I want. If that makes me a [deleted], okay!⁵ **❞**
>
> — **Madonna, early 90s**

For Further Study:
Read Proverbs 31:10-31. Which aspects of the Proverbs 31 woman would be most acceptable in our culture? Which would be least acceptable?

> **❝** I am responsible for courting that fame, but I didn't know what I was getting myself into. I convinced myself that it was going to be enough to take the place of real intimacy. I was incredibly naive. Part of it was just being young and having fun. The other part was a lonely young girl's longing and search to be fulfilled.⁷ **❞**
>
> — **Madonna, 1998**

Gurley Brown, for 31 years editor of *Cosmopolitan*, is radically different in view and constituency from Patricia Ireland, yet in a recent interview she comments regarding why she wanted to run Cosmo: "I really knew from the very first hour what I wanted to say and who I wanted to write for—that 23-year-old with her nose pressed to the glass, not having everything, and wanting more, and willing to try hard for it....[The Cosmo Girl] wants to do it better, she wants to have it all."⁶

The Militant Feminist and the sassy Cosmo Girl are both adamant about what they want, it's just that they want quite different things. One defines her wants in terms of an independent identity, the other in terms of the culture of beauty. The modern woman is constantly pulled between these two mutually incompatible goals. For every *Ms. Magazine* there is a *Mademoiselle*. For every book on how to compete with a man there's one on how to keep him. Both views, however, define womanhood unbiblically, because they define it in external terms. They falsely claim that the truly modern woman can only find meaning in how she looks or what she controls.

---

2 Read 1 Timothy 2:9-10. Write one phrase each to describe how you will express modesty in:

Dress:

Speech:

Behavior toward men:

The biblical picture is quite different. The Bible portrays true femininity not as external assertiveness or attractiveness, but as something that is fundamentally internal. Biblical femininity is a conquest of the heart and a beauty of the soul. Scripture's instruction to women emphasizes qualities such as reverence, self-control, purity, and kindness. Peter instructs women that, "Your beauty should not come from outward adornment....Instead it should be that of your inner self, the unfading beauty of a gentle and quiet spirit, which is of great worth in God's sight" (1Pe 3:3-4).

Is Peter saying the godly woman is to be seen and not heard? Or that women can only be godly when devoid of all adornment? No! Peter is encouraging women that the audience that really matters is an audience of One. The Bible provides women with wisdom that is timeless and fully relevant for today. In a world that would limit your vision to the superficial and external, the woman of God fulfills her call from the inside out. The great examples of women in the Scriptures—Deborah, Ruth, Hannah, Esther, Mary, and others—all exhibit this character, regardless of the task to which they were called. These women were not foolish, rebellious, or vain. They demonstrated true loveliness by being prepared in heart for the time and task of God's choosing.

The fight for power and position that consumes the feminist woman, and the lust for fashion that enslaves the worldly woman, are both enticements to the Christian woman. Who wouldn't be tempted to seek to "do it better, and have it all"? But at what cost?

The church is made up of women and men working in complementary relationship. In its ideal state this relationship, through a balance of outer impact and inner fire, produces a church strong in mission and deep in passion for God. But where lust for power or obsession with beauty is present among its women, the church is hindered in its passion for the Lord.

In the Scriptures the idea of a flame is often used to signify God's presence. The flame of God's presence led the children of Israel through the wilderness. The Spirit

> ❝ Women in the 1890s might have compared themselves with the other ten girls their age in the village. Women in the 1990s must compare themselves with pictures of the cream of the worldwide modeling industry. The images peer out from every magazine cover: men's magazines teach men what to look *for*, and women's magazines teach women what to look *like*.[8] ❞
>
> **— David Powlison**

For Further Study:
Read Judges 4:1-10. How did Deborah acknowledge the distinctive leadership responsibilities of men and women in her interaction with Barak?

INNER ADORNMENT—THE FRUIT OF THE SPIRIT

One of the greatest challenges women face in the pursuit of godliness is the temptation to focus on outward appearance. This is not a new problem. First Peter 3:3-4 warns women not to evaluate their beauty by "outward adornment," but instead by the "inner self, the unfading beauty of a gentle and quiet spirit." Paul's description of this inner quality is the fruit of the Spirit (Gal 5:22-23). While men and women should both desire to produce this fruit, it can be particularly helpful to women in their battle against the cultural obsession with outward striving or adornment. The following definitions of the fruit of the Spirit may be helpful to meditate on.[9]

Love—a sacrificial commitment to the welfare of another person regardless of that person's response, and regardless of what he or she might give me in return.

Joy—a deep, abiding, inner thankfulness to God for his goodness, that remains uninterrupted when less desirable circumstances of life intrude.

Peace—a heartfelt tranquility and trust that does not disappear during the storms of life, because it is anchored in the overwhelming consciousness that I am in the hand of God.

Patience—a quality of self-restraint that does not retaliate in the midst of provoking situations.

Kindness—a sensitive awareness and willingness to seek out ways in which to serve others.

Goodness—an unswerving capacity to deal with people rightly as God defines that term, even when they need correction.

Faithfulness—an inner loyalty that results in remaining true to my spiritual convictions and commitments.

Gentleness—controlled strength dispensed from a humble heart.

Self-control—an inward personal mastery that submits my desires to the greater cause of God's will.

of God came upon the Christians at Pentecost as a flame. A flame represents power, purity, and light. A flame also requires tending and care. The five wise maidens in the parable made sure their torches were ready, and that the flame stayed lit. How can you as a Christian single woman follow the example of the wise maidens, and care for the lamp of God's presence in your life and sphere of influence?

Tend the flame. Have you ever walked with a candle through a dark and drafty house? You learn quickly to protect the flame from the elements, or risk having it go out on you (typically, right after you hear a creepy noise in the next room). The tending of a flame is not done with bold gestures or impulsive activity, for as strong as fire can rage, it can also flicker and fade. Tending a flame requires patience, attention to detail, and a wisdom to know that the stronger the flame, the farther the light will push back the darkness.

Meditate on 2 Kings 4:1-7. What can you learn from the widow about how to handle a sense of inadequacy or lack?

How can you, like a wise maiden, tend the flame? First of all, don't let the howling winds of cultural change blow out your fire. Be a woman of the Word, and let the Bible define you, not the feminist movement or the fashion world. Study what Scripture says about you, and value its wisdom for your life. Recognize that stirring dying coals and fanning promising sparks in the church demands character. Discontent, double-mindedness, worldliness, and the like produce impatience with God and his plan for your life. In the end, your eternal reward will not be for the ministries you ran or the spiritual gifts you used, but for the lives you touched. A woman who perseveres in her distinctive calling in God will fan the flame of faith in the hearts of many, and will be of great value to the work of God in her generation.

> **❝** Zeal, as you know, means an earnest, ardent desire, giving rise to a correspondent energy of action, to obtain some favourite object; and when directed to a right object is a noble and elevated state of mind....It is like fire, which may be applied to many useful purposes when under wise direction, but which if not kept in its proper place and under proper restraint may cause a conflagration....The zeal that is likely to be continuous, to honour God, to do good to our fellow-creatures, is that which is cherished in the closet of devotion, fed by the oil of Scripture, and fanned by the breath of prayer.[10] **❞**
>
> **— John Angell James**

In Acts 16 Paul travels to Philippi. There he meets Lydia, a successful businesswoman who happens to be single. Whether she was ever married, we don't know. We

For Further Study:
Read the account of Ruth (see book of Ruth). How did she exercise godliness in facing hardship?

do know that she is "a worshiper of God" (v. 14) and that she received the gospel, becoming the first Christian in that part of the world! Her home became the meeting place for the church in Philippi, and her gift of hospitality became one of the great marks of this church that Paul loved so dearly. Lydia's faith fanned the flame of a church that Paul considered his "partners in the gospel" (Php 1:5). Lydia was a single woman of influence, grace, and passion for God.

---

3 Read the account of Anna (Luke 2:36-38) and Mary of Bethany (John 12:1-7). Write three words that describe their devotion.

-

-

-

Fan the flame. Don't be content just to keep the fire burning—fan the flame! Disciplines like prayer, evangelism, worship, and servanthood will both increase your zeal and inspire others to greater passion in God. For example, Debbie is a single sister in our church, and a highly successful manager in a national company. Is she known in the church for her business leadership? No, and she doesn't seek to be. She is known for prayer. She is an intercessor who regularly gathers folks at her home for times of prayer. Sylvia is a single woman in another church. She is a banker who doesn't let that often dry profession rob her radiant joy. She loves the lost with her life, and attracts them with her spirit.

These women contribute in many other ways, but their primary vision is that the church maintain a burden for the lost and a heart for God. I don't know where we'd be without them and the many others like them. Deb and Sylvia are doing more than tending the fire, they're fanning the flame in themselves, and warming us all in the glow.

Meditate on Acts 9:36-43. Do you think that Dorcas was important to the church in Joppa? Why?

Pass the Torch. Hannah More was a woman of extraordinary talents. An accomplished playwright, she traveled in the best circles of London society in the late 1700s. Her faith was sincere, but carefully adapted to her secular lifestyle. The deaths of some of her closest friends shook her and sent her on a quest to understand the faith of her childhood. In time she found her friends changing, and her heart as well. She met people who were serious about applying their faith to real-life dilemmas, and they lovingly challenged her to do the same. Encouraged by her new pastor, John Newton (who wrote the hymn "Amazing Grace"), she caught a vision. God had given her intelligence, gifting, position, and wealth, and she wanted to spend it all for him.

Initially her "consecrated pen" became her ministry, and she produced many widely read tracts, dramas, and essays addressing the problems of the day from a Christian perspective. Her writings helped stem the tide in England of a revolutionary anarchy that had already devastated France. With her longtime friend William Wilberforce she helped overthrow slavery in England. She became one of the most important benefactors to the ministries of John and Charles Wesley.

In time she and her sisters developed a burden for the poor and, venturing out of their comfortable upper-class surroundings, created an education and evangelism program in one of London's poorest areas. Yet Hannah More also was deeply committed to the discipling of young women in the faith, serving them with her pen and her life. She became the most influential woman in England, even though she never held a position in any power structure.

> 66 We are apt to mistake our vocation by looking out of the way for occasions to exercise great and rare virtues, and by stepping over the ordinary ones that lie directly in the road before us.[11] 99
>
> — Hannah More

Meditate on Proverbs 14. How can you be building up your house? How could you be tearing it down?

---

4 Read Paul's closing greetings in Romans 16:1-16. What do Mary, Tryphena, Tryphosa, and Persis have in common?

❏ They are all supermodels

❏ They have the same first names as The Supremes

❏ They were Paul's travel agents

❏ They were notable for their hard work for the gospel

What made Hannah More special? She had vision for a life beyond personal accomplishment. She worked within the biblical limits of her gifting and calling. She had a commitment to her local Christian community that nourished her faith. She was obedient to the promptings of God. She expressed her trust in God through the giving of her resources and life. She took Paul's admonition to "train younger women" (Tit 2:3-4) seriously. In short, not only did she fan the flame in her life and her church, she gave her life to passing it on beyond her generation and social group.

> A woman who is unmarried has the ability, by God's grace, to honor God in her single life. If she can bring glory to God now, she can do it for life.[12]
>
> — Lorrie Skowronski

We have a number of Hannah Mores in our church, any one of whom could carve out an impressive individual ministry for herself. But each is having a far greater impact by embracing the womanly call to stir up the fire of God in the midst of his people.

Every Christian single woman has the opportunity to be a Lydia or a Hannah More. The temptations to give in to the culture are real, and the choices you make are crucial. Which world will you live in, which Kingdom will have your allegiance? Let me leave you to ponder this with the hard-won wisdom of Amy Carmichael:

> We who love our Lord, and we whose affections are set on the things that are heaven for us *today*—we voluntarily and gladly lay aside things that charm the world, so that we may be charmed and ravished with the things of heaven. Then our whole being may be poured forth in constant and unreserved devotion in serving our Lord, who died to save us....We are called to live daily in a higher Kingdom, where we are touched, and our souls drink from the Spirit of God.[13]

Single Men: Carry the Colors

I am a history buff with an intense interest in the Civil War. I particularly enjoy visiting the battlefield parks of major engagements of the war. Although not a fan of war itself, I find myself deeply moved when standing in the midst of a battlefield and realizing this is where men gave their lives for something greater than themselves. I can spend all day reading monuments and plaques. A life goal is to read all 5000 monuments at Gettysburg; I have about 3000 left.

One of the most beautifully preserved battlefields is

> " At the heart of mature masculinity is a sense of benevolent responsibility to lead, provide for, and protect women in ways appropriate to a man's differing relationships.[14] "
>
> — John Piper

For Further Study:
Read Isaiah 11:10-12. What is the prophetic significance of banner imagery?

Meditate on Exodus 17:8-16. Who was most important in the defeat of the Amalekites: Joshua? Moses? Or Aaron and Hur?

Antietam, site of the bloodiest day of fighting of the Civil War. The Antietam visitor's center holds an amazing painting of a group of soldiers battling around a regimental flag. Regimental flags were the individual banners or "colors" of a regiment that distinguished that group of soldiers from all others. The ultimate colors of the army were the national flags—the Stars and Stripes of the Union, and the Stars and Bars of the Confederacy. The picture in the visitor's center so fascinated me that I did some study on the purpose and use of flags and banners throughout history.

Banners and flags provide identity and direction to large groups of people who need to move in a coordinated way. In the Old Testament, the people were counted and organized by tribe and family under banners (Nu 2:1-2, 34). As the Israelites wandered in the desert, each evening the banners were planted around the tabernacle in precise array, enabling the people to transform themselves from a mob into a community of faith. Under these banners the nation traveled and arrayed in battle. The banners identified one's place of belonging in times of peace, and provided a rallying point in times of war. In Exodus 17, Moses himself became a human regimental flag: the Israelites were able to defeat the Amalekites only when Moses' hands were held aloft. But Moses, realizing it was not his power that won the day, dedicated an altar named "The Lord is My Banner." For Israel, a banner was a sign of God's sovereign control, intervention, and identification with his people.

How does all this apply to single men? Let's face it, the sexual revolution has done a number on guys. The traditional ideas of masculinity are under siege from every side. Men are told that to reclaim their identity they need to do everything from primal screaming in the woods to exploring their feminine side as if it were some recently discovered treasure island. Not surprisingly, this confusion has filtered into the church.

But I believe there is a clear call to masculinity for the Christian single man. The biblical call for single men can be expressed in the opportunity to "carry the colors" in the church. But what does this mean?

Sacrifice. Throughout history, the great honor of being selected to carry the colors of the army has gone to that soldier who was both totally trustworthy and

CARRYING THE COLORS—NOT FOR THE FAINT OF HEART

Some of the greatest gallantry of the Civil War was exhibited in the protection of or assault on the colors or regimental banners. The following are a few actual examples of soldiers who knew the life and death symbolism of the battle flag.

- A New York Regiment was surrounded and about to be overrun when the color bearer, instead of retreating, went out into the open in front of the troops and planted the flag, inspiring the troops to charge the startled enemy and drive them off the field of battle.

- At the battle of Cedar Mountain, General Stonewall Jackson saw his troops running from the battle. He grabbed the colors himself and carried them to the front, causing his troops to stop, turn around, and resume fighting.

- At the battle of Gettysburg, nine color bearers of the 24th Michigan regiment were shot and 14 of the 26th North Carolina Regiment were shot in a single day's fighting. The last man to die carrying the colors that day for the 26th NC had wrapped the colors around himself to keep them from falling into enemy hands. He lost his life, the flag was saved.

- Joshua Chamberlain, one of the great heroes of the Civil War, picked up the colors of his regiment when they had fallen during the battle of Petersburg and held them aloft for the troops to rally around. He was shot through both hips, and when he couldn't stand on his own, stuck his sword in the ground and leaned against it in order to keep the colors flying.

- The 54th Massachusetts Regiment, the first black fighting regiment in U.S. history, suffered more than 50 percent casualties in an unsuccessful effort to storm a confederate fort in South Carolina. Sgt. William Carney bore the colors that day and was wounded several times in the battle, yet as he was carried off the field his words to his defeated comrades were, "Don't worry, the old flag never touched the ground'." Sgt Carney became the first black recipient of the Medal of Honor. The "Fighting 54th" was immortalized in the film, *Glory*.

- At the Battle of Antietam one particularly zealous color bearer was found standing in the open waving the flag furiously in the air. When asked what he was doing he said, "Need to get some bullet holes in it. Ain't no good without bullet holes!"

extremely brave—for he who carries the colors has no hand free to carry a gun. Maleness in our day, by contrast, is all about attitude and image. I see it in the locker room of the gym I frequently (well, occasionally) attend: guys preening in front of mirrors, talking trash about women, complaining about their bosses. Rebellious attitudes, slackerism, fatalism, rowdyism, materialism, and the like all speak of a lack of sustaining vision or mission for our maleness. While still at the top of the social power structure, men are taking hits on all sides, and are deserting their positions of influence in the culture wars. We have become fans of everything, but participants in little that ultimately matters.

Meditate on Daniel 1:3-20. What are some of the peer pressures that Daniel and his friends might have experienced?

Contrast this with the vision of single man Paul, as expressed in these excerpts from his letter to a persecuted church in Philippi:

> Because of my chains, most of the brothers in the Lord have been encouraged to speak the Word of God more courageously and fearlessly....For to me, to live is Christ and to die is gain....But even if I am being poured out like a drink offering on the sacrifice and service coming from your faith, I am glad and rejoice with all of you....Whatever was to my profit I now consider loss for the sake of Christ....I want to know Christ and the power of his resurrection and the fellowship of sharing in his sufferings....Forgetting what is behind and straining toward what is ahead, I press on toward the goal (Php 1:14, 21; 2:17; 3:7, 10, 13-14).

5 In 2 Timothy 2:1-7, Paul gives three good pictures of how the godly man should live. Complete the following sentences with your own application.

Like a soldier, I will _____

Like an athlete, I will _____

Like a farmer, I will _____

Paul could have played it safe, made a name for himself. But he gave it up for a greater cause—something beyond himself. He embraced sacrifice as his lifestyle. The bearer of the colors knows that his is a lonely position, in the middle of the fray, unable to defend himself. Yet he presses on, because he knows that when he took the honor of the cause in his hands he gave away his right to think only of himself. He became a caretaker of the reality that there is more to the battle than survival. He gives himself wholly for the goal, knowing that others will follow his example.

How, in practical terms, can a single man live this sacrificial life? Let me tell you about Fred and Ed. Fred is Mr. Faithful on our sound team. He has been there for years, serving in obscurity, the first to be at the meetings and the last to leave. Ed serves on the parking team, rain or shine, helping people find spaces in the crowded parking lot. He also runs our nursing-home ministry, taking a team of folks out on Sundays to visit the elderly.

So what's the big deal? Well, Fred also happens to be an owner of a prestigious engineering firm downtown. Ed also happens to teach biblical studies at the graduate level. Fred and Ed could have traded on their personal accomplishments for prominence in the church. Instead they took up the banner of servanthood, and are calling others to follow.

> **66** The crisis of belief is a turning point or a fork in the road that demands that you make a decision. You must decide what you believe about God. How you respond when you reach this turning point will determine whether you go on to be involved with God in something God-sized that only He can do or whether you will continue to go your own way and miss what God has purposed for your life. This is not a one-time experience. It is a daily experience. How you live your life is a testimony of what you believe about God.[16] **99**
>
> — **Henry Blackaby, Claude King**

How can you live the sacrificial life? How about by not letting your job dictate your life? Leave the carrot of the career fast-track for someone else to grope at. How about by learning to babysit? Or by trading some nights in front of the tube for serious study of Scripture? How about helping a single mother rake her leaves? How about developing fewer opinions and more questions? You get the idea.

Responsibility. In 1961, the USS Thresher nuclear submarine sank with 129 crew members aboard. The commander of the nuclear navy, Admiral Hyman Rickover, was summoned to Congress and asked to assess blame for

For Further Study:
Psalm 51:16-17. What heart attitude will produce sacrifice that is acceptable to God?

the disaster. A strong leader, he had not only developed the nuclear program, but had butted heads with politicians over it for years. He knew he had enemies who were seeking to exact revenge. When asked to give his opinion as to what had gone wrong, he could have easily blamed any number of technical or human factors, but he shouldered the blame himself. In his testimony he explained,

> Responsibility is a unique concept: it can only reside and inhere in a single individual. You may share it with others, but your portion is not diminished. You may delegate it, but it is still with you. You may disclaim it, but you cannot divest yourself of it. Even if you do not recognize or admit its presence, you cannot escape it. If responsibility is rightfully yours, no evasion, or ignorance, or passing the blame can shift the burden to someone else. Unless you can point your finger at the man who is responsible when something goes wrong, then you have never had anyone really responsible.[17]

Read that again and ponder it. What the admiral defined as responsibility, in older times was known as duty. For duty men often went to war, and sometimes to prison. For duty men told the truth, and men respected women. To carry the colors in a parade was an honor. To carry the colors in battle was duty. Sadly, the concept of duty is as out of favor in our day as is the idea of driving the speed limit.

Meditate on John 21:15-19, Acts 2:14-41. What do these passages tell you about God's ability to help us do what we are called to do?

Faith is a prerequisite of duty. That's why duty is never about doing things out of guilt. A man oriented to duty recognizes that nothing of consequence gets done unless someone puts himself on the line. Nehemiah was brokenhearted about the desolation of Jerusalem, but what set him apart was that he did something about it. It involved risk and hardship, but he saw that the occasion needed a man. He sought the Lord, heard God's call, and did his duty. Are you looking for fresh challenges in God, or are you bunkered down in survival mode? In an age where men avoid responsibility like it's a polyester leisure suit, a single man who is grace-motivated and duty-bound can make a difference in this world.

Resolve. The man carrying the colors was always included in the battle plan. He was told of the objective, and was to press on toward that objective with all diligence. He couldn't get caught up in the fray or turn back. He must lead on toward the goal. He was the focus of the advance. All the troops fell in behind him. At the same time, he was the focal point of the attack, for the enemy knew that if the color-bearer could be cut down, his fellow troops could be routed in the confusion.

Facing the full fury of battle and unable to defend himself or retreat, the color-bearer knew that he was the source of hope amid calamity in battle. When the banner was lost, hope was lost. But as long as the banner was flying, there was reason to continue the fight. One color-bearer at Antietam described the dilemma of being the focal point of both attack and hope: "Between the physical fear of going forward and the moral fear of going backward, there is a predicament of exceptional awkwardness."[19]

> ❝ It is around the standard bearer that the fight is thickest. There the battle-axes ring upon the helmets and the arrows are bent upon the armor, for the foe knows that if he can cut down the standard, he will strike a heavy blow and cause deep discouragement.[18] ❞
>
> — Charles Spurgeon

Single brothers, this "exceptional awkwardness" is real to you, I am sure. The fight can seem overwhelming, and tangible reward for the effort can seem scarce. Resolve is the faith that keeps you moving even when the fog of battle overwhelms you. Jesus had resolve in going to the Cross. Paul had resolve in pressing on toward the goal. Resolve looks ahead. Resolve is clear-eyed, level-headed, sober-thinking. It is fueled by the burning reality that service in this life is the only battle that matters, and that God himself has placed you in it. So spend it all here. As the famous missionary motto proclaims, "No retreat, no surrender, no reserve."

For Further Study:
Matthew 26:31-46. In what ways did Jesus have to express resolve in this passage?

God made you a man for a purpose. Inherent in your masculinity is a call to step forward, not simply to take the flag, but first to ask for it and reach toward it. Masculinity is the raw material of leadership in God's government, but you don't need to wait for a tap on the shoulder to express your innate leadership call. You can lead by influence and example. If you are not being trained to lead, get your Bible out and train yourself! Your Christian single sisters are always looking for men to step out in leadership in areas such as purity, discernment, decisions, and godly conversation. Like Nehemiah, the only things you need to make a real impact are a willingness to sacrifice, the faith to do your duty, and resolve to finish the task.

Men and women, weary of fighting the battles of the gender wars, are yearning for peace. Christian men and women who relish the roles and responsibilities that God has given can provide a way out of the confusion. The beauty of God's way is that whether your singles group is counted by the hundreds or by the handful, you can be a compelling example of the richness of biblical manhood and womanhood if you embrace your distinctive call.

Sisters, fan the flame. Brothers, carry the colors. Be the Church! ■

GROUP DISCUSSION

1. What has most shaped your views of the opposite sex?

2. How can Christians remain true to biblical standards while reaching out to those with different social views?

3. How important is it that we try to change the way our society deals with moral issues?

4. What well-known personality currently represents the cultural ideal of womanhood? Why?

5. What well-known personality currently represents the cultural ideal of manhood? Why?

6. What are some ways in your local church where women can fan the flame of the church?

7. What are some obstacles that single men will face if they pick up the banner in the church?

8. Reread the quote from Admiral Rickover on page 49. Which of the ways to avoid responsibility described in the quote are a temptation for you?

9. Have you had a moment of "exceptional awkwardness" like the one described by the flag carrier? What caused it?

Answers to Warm-Up
(from page 33):

National Organization of Women begins, 1966

Billie Jean King beats Bobby Riggs in the Battle of the Sexes (Tennis Version), 1973

Susan B. Anthony Dollar introduced, 1979

Ms. Pac-Man becomes more popular as a video game than Pac-Man, 1982

Ellen DeGeneres: The closet episode, 1997

RECOMMENDED READING

Recovering Biblical Manhood and Womanhood edited by John Piper and Wayne Grudem (Wheaton, IL: Crossway Books, 1991)

Christians in the Wake of the Sexual Revolution by Randy Alcorn (Portland, OR: Multnomah Press, 1985)

Spiritual Leadership by J. Oswald Sanders (Chicago, IL: Moody Press, 1980)

Let Me Be a Woman by Elisabeth Elliot (Wheaton, IL: Tyndale House Publishers, 1976)

RICH IN WISDOM

Strategy: The rich single life develops a faith that roots below the topsoil of culture and circumstance, yielding the fruit of good decisions and a hunger to obey God.

BIBLE STUDY Isaiah 33:6

WARM-UP Draw lines to match the following philosophers with the worldy-wise sound bite for which each is famous.

René Descartes •
    • "Man is condemned to be free"

Sören Kierkegaard •
    • "I think, therefore I am"

Karl Marx •
    • "Truth is subjectivity"

Jean Paul Sartre •
    • "Religion is the opiate of the people"

(See page 70 for answers)

PERSONAL STUDY Seven a.m. at the IHOP. Maybe not the first place you'd think of going to sort out life's thorny questions, but there we were. The guy sitting across from my blueberry pancakes was wrestling with a dilemma that is not unusual for the single Christian men and women I know.

"I need to find a new place to live," he told me. "Right now I live close to my job, but not to any of my friends. If I move close to my friends, I'll have a long commute to work and not have time to do anything with anybody. If I stay close to my job, I keep the short commute, but I'll still be too far away to get together with people during the week. Not only that, I'm wondering if I should get a place by myself, or live with some other guys. Do I keep renting or do I try to invest in a house? I just wish I knew God's will!"

As the questions tumbled out all over our breakfast, it became apparent that no one question stood alone—each was connected to other questions. Where to begin? What

Meditate on James 4:13-15. What are some things you do that you just assume are God's will?

was the key strand in this tangled mess that would unravel the mystery of God's will for my friend? I looked down at my pancakes, which had not only soaked up all my syrup, but any simple answers I might have offered as well.

Wrestling with the Will of God

This sincere brother did not need to wash down his breakfast with a theological discussion on the nature of God's will. We could have taken most of the morning to reflect on God's sovereign will and moral will, his necessary will and his free will, and his secret will and revealed will. Such distinctions can be tremendously helpful in understanding how God, in his providence, works in our lives. But what about the other side of the equation? How do we follow God in day-to-day decisions? When confronted with our limited perspective, and confused by our mixed motives, can we truly know and obey God's will?

This question can be particularly challenging for single men and women. For the single adult, the freedom to live in undistracted devotion to God brings a perplexing array of decisions and lifestyle choices. By comparison, marriage and family tend to simplify decision-making by narrowing one's range of options. What I do with everything from my money to my weekends is processed through the grid of my roles as husband and parent.

Say I need a car. I may love that new sport-utility vehicle... but I'll take the used mini-van. It's a no-brainer for Andy Husband-Father. But if I were single, I'd more likely be able to take the sport-utility vehicle *or* the mini-van. No wonder advertisers target families for basic items like insurance and detergents (and mini-vans), while the ads for luxury items such as sports cars, stereos, and cruises tend to feature single people. Advertisers know that most married people see their decisions in terms of necessity, while single people are more likely to interpret decisions in terms of opportunity.

> **"** Belief that divine guidance is real rests upon two foundation-facts: first, the reality of God's *plan* for us; second, the ability of God to *communicate* with us.[1] **"**
>
> — **J.I. Packer**

The question my single friend wrestled with, therefore, was not the mountain-top question of "What is the will of God?" It was an intensely practical question: "How can I

For Further Study:
Read Genesis 13. What motivated Lot in his decision? What motivated Abram?

evaluate the opportunities in my life and make good decisions about them?" In the end, however, the heart cry of my single friends is not merely to go through life compiling a resume of good choices. Underlying their day-to-day concerns is a burning desire to walk the path of life under the guidance of God, and to please him both in the decisions they make, and how they go about making them.

In the final analysis, it is a heart cry for wisdom.

---

1 Which of the following best describes the way you make decisions?

❏ If I wait long enough this problem will get bored and go away

❏ Analysis is next to godliness

❏ Decide first, ask questions later

❏ I'll give you five dollars if you make this decision for me

---

Is Anyone Asking?

In his epistle, the apostle James responds to this cry: "If any of you lacks wisdom, he should ask God, who gives generously to all without finding fault, and it will be given to him" (1:5). When we think of wisdom, we may think it's something we amass over time, like gray hair. Or we may think wisdom is only gained through lifelong study or mystical experiences. But James looks at people needing wisdom for ordinary perplexities and says, "You need it, ask for it."

> ### J.I. PACKER ON WISDOM
>
> Wisdom is the power to see, and the inclination to choose, the best and highest goal, together with the surest means of attaining it.[2]
>
> Wisdom in Scripture means choosing the best and noblest end at which to aim, along with the most appropriate and effective means to it.[3]

Not only does God respond, he *delights* to give wisdom. Commentator Alec Motyer describes the literal understanding of God's intentions in this verse: "This is how the 'giving God' gives—with a selfless, total concern for us and with an exclusive preoccupation as if he had nothing else to do but to give and give again."[4] God isn't miserly

For Further Study:
Read James 1:5-8. What causes us to be unstable in our decision-making?

with his precious pearls of wisdom. He backs up the truck and dumps wisdom into the lives of those who ask in faith. But what is this "wisdom" that God so desires to send our way?

The concept of wisdom has been around for ages. Nearly every ancient culture had extensive wisdom literature. Does this make wisdom the franchise of white-robed philosophers or proverb-spouting gurus? Not at all.

Meditate on Proverbs 11:2, 13:10. How can pride affect our ability to make good decisions?

The Bible provides a perspective on wisdom that is incredibly practical. James admonishes his readers, "Who is wise and understanding among you? Let him show it by his good life, by deeds done in the humility that comes from wisdom" (3:13). The biblical treasure of wisdom, the Book of Proverbs, promises that with wisdom comes protection (2:11); long life (3:16); peace (3:17); honor (4:9); a steady walk (4:10-12); prosperity (19:8); patience (19:11) and a host of other practical benefits. But where does wisdom come from?

The first thing to know about wisdom is that it is not some force out there in the universe that we tap into. God, "the only wise" (Ro 16:27), is both the source of wisdom and the barometer by which it is measured. James contrasts the wisdom that "comes from heaven" with that which is "earthly, unspiritual, of the devil" (Jas 3:15). Paul contrasts God's wisdom with "man's wisdom," which is foolish by comparison (1Co 1:22-31).

> ❝ Oh, the depth of the riches of the wisdom and knowledge of God! How unsearchable his judgments, and his paths beyond tracing out! Who has known the mind of the Lord? Or who has been his counselor? Who has ever given to God, that God should repay him? For from him and through him and to him are all things. To him be the glory forever! Amen.[5] ❞
>
> **— Paul the Apostle**

The purest view we have of God's wisdom is in Jesus Christ, "in whom are hidden all the treasures of wisdom and knowledge" (Col 2:3). When wisdom needed a face, it was not that of Buddha, Socrates, or Jim Morrison, but of Jesus Christ, "Who became for us wisdom from God" (1Co 2:26). Biblical wisdom involves interaction between the God of wisdom and those who come to him for it.

Meditate on 1 Corinthians 10:22-31. What foolishness has Christ removed from your life since you have known him?

Wayne Grudem defines God's wisdom as his ability to always choose the best goals and the best means to attain those goals.[6] According to James, this is essentially what we get for the asking from God! The *New Bible Dictionary* defines wisdom as "forming the correct plan to gain the desired results....Wisdom takes insights gleaned from the knowledge of God's ways and applies them in the daily walk."[7] But does this mean that wisdom is simply figuring out the best way to get what we want? Not in the least!

---

2 Which of the following sources of wisdom would you consult if nobody was around to notice?

❑ Daily Horoscope   ❑ Ann Landers/Dear Abby

❑ Radio call-in shows   ❑ Other:

The essential difference between God and man is that he is holy and we are not. His motives are always purely good, ours are always mixed (at best). In order for wisdom to be communicated to us, it has to affect not only what we do, but the inclination of our hearts as well. John Wesley prayed: "Give me, O Lord, that highest learning, to know thee; and that best wisdom, to know myself."[8] John Calvin, who would find considerable debate with Wesley on a number of fronts, echoes this prayer: "Our wisdom, in so far as it ought to be deemed true and solid Wisdom, consists almost entirely of two parts: the knowledge of God and of ourselves."[9]

For Further Study:
Read James 3:13-18. List the words from verse 17 that describe heavenly wisdom. Next to each word, write its earthly and unspiritual counterpart.

What these two giants of the faith are telling us is crucial to our understanding of wisdom. When it comes to wisdom, the rightness (or righteousness) of our character is as much an issue as is the quality of our decisions. God's wisdom will not only reveal the best course of action, it will teach us about ourselves in light of his holiness. As David reflects in Psalm 51:6, "Surely you desire truth in the inner parts, you teach wisdom in the inmost place." Wisdom from God is meant to affect our decisions and our hearts alike.

How can we begin to operate in wisdom in both the big decisions and the day-to-day steps of the single life? I would like to offer three essential tools for appropriating the wisdom God gives. They are Doctrine, Discipline, and Direction.

For Further Study:
Read Isaiah 6:1-10. What is most fearful about Isaiah's vision?

Doctrine: An Education in Fear

"The fear of the LORD is the beginning of wisdom, and knowledge of the Holy One is understanding" (Pr 9:10). We know from this familiar verse that wisdom is somehow connected to the way we understand God. But what is "the fear of the Lord"?

> **"** Fearing God is not a negative experience for those who love God. It is the kind of deeply satisfying trembling, and sweet humility and submission that rises in the presence of the absolute power and holiness of God....The safest place in the universe is with our arms around the neck of God. And the most dangerous place is any path where we flee from his presence.[13] **"**
>
> **— John Piper**

Calvin described it as "reverence mingled with honor and fear."[10] Puritan theologian Charles Bridges called it "that affectionate reverence, by which the child of God bends himself humbly and carefully to his Father's law."[11] More recently, Sinclair Ferguson has described it as a "right recognition of God."[12] Simply put, the fear of the Lord is a right understanding of God that allows us to relate properly to him.

I'd like to toss a couple of terms in here: theology and doctrine. Do you know the difference? Here are some clues.

Theology is simply the study of God. You study God–you're proving it just by reading this book! So congratulations: you're a theologian (no, the term does *not* apply exclusively to full-time seminary professors). *Doctrine* is the way we organize the different aspects of our theology for practical use. It is the mental files and folders we put our theological ideas into. Maybe you couldn't write a book about your doctrine, but that's not the point. Doctrine is your attempt to apply theology (what you believe about God) to everyday life.

How important is doctrine? The *first* thing recorded in Scripture about the *first* Christian church is that they were devoted to the doctrine of the apostles (Ac 2:37-42). Every church that received a New Testament letter was instructed in doctrine. The emphasis in Scripture is on "sound doctrine" (Tit 2:1). This literally means "hygienic" doctrine—clean, healthy, and uncluttered. Conversely, *un*sound doctrine is messy, polluted, and unhealthy. The way we understand God in practical terms through doctrine will affect how we relate to God and his will for our lives.

Meditate on Psalm 119: 1-8. How should your doctrine affect your behavior?

When I worked in real estate, I "organized" my desk by piling everything on top of it and digging around until I found what I needed. Occasionally I would throw some things away (like old candy-bar wrappers), but most of the time my desk was covered by a precarious mound of paper. Whenever my desk was clear I would get scared that something had been lost, so I kept everything in big piles on the desk—so it would be lost in a confined space. Was this the best system of organization? No, but I was comfortable with it. The only time my system failed me was when I needed it most: when I had to find something right away.

It's much the same with doctrine. Our doctrine can be cluttered with inconsistencies and error, and we may not even be aware of it. It's when we need to act on it, in the midst of a tough decision or difficult trial, that the "soundness" of our doctrine is tested.

Let's say I believe the unsound doctrine that God guarantees me a smooth day whenever I start the morning in prayer. Then one day, I pray in the morning but have a really difficult day anyway. What happens then? If I truly believe that unsound doctrine, I will start to question whether God really cares or knows about me. I will begin to doubt that prayer has any benefit. My unsound doctrine has not only failed me for today, it has led me down a path to other unsound doctrines that are far more damaging. Sound doctrine, on the other hand, will always lead me to an accurate understanding of God and my place in his plan. Sound doctrine provides vital perspective in times of decision.

How do we "clean up" our doctrine? By allowing the pure washing of God's Word, the Bible, to expose the impurities and errors in our understanding of God. Though we can encounter God and his truth in many ways, all of our experiences and assumptions must pass the test of Scripture. Theologian Bruce Milne states, "Getting doctrine right is the key to getting everything else right. If we are to know who God is, who we are, and what God wants of us, we need to study Scripture."[15]

For Further Study:
Read 1 Timothy 1:3-11. What do false doctrines promote? What does sound doctrine promote?

> 66 [Scripture] is given to make us humble, holy, wise in spiritual things; to direct us in our duties, to relieve us in our temptations, to comfort us under troubles, to make us love God and live unto Him.[14] 99
>
> — John Owen

How does sound doctrine help us gain wisdom? By causing us to fear God with the right kind of fear. When we think of God rightly, we will fear him rightly. We begin to see that there is no inconsistency between the holiness of God our Judge and the love of God our Father. We begin to be thankful that his ways are higher than our ways (Isa 55:9). Sound doctrine helps us better understand God's character, and this draws out trust from us, the way the faithful love of a parent stirs up trust in a child. We learn to pray with confidence, and act in faith. In the midst of perplexities of life, sound doctrine allows us to appreciate and rest in a holy fear of God.

---

3 The fear of God has been described as a holy terror. Which of the following nightmares would provoke unholy fear in you?

❏ Being chased by someone but stuck in one spot

❏ Walking into work or school only to discover that all you have on is underwear

❏ Falling off a cliff

❏ Being an hour late for the final exam of the class you need to graduate

---

When Shadrach, Meshach, and Abednego faced the toughest decision of their lives, whether to bow down to idols or be thrown into the fire, they did not have time for prayer, study, or a quick call to the local Bible answer man. They only had what they knew of God and his ways. Their response is an inspiring example of sound doctrine—men living in holy and uncompromising fear of the Lord:

> **❝** There is one thing you have spoken
> There are two things I have found
> You O Lord are ever loving
> You O Lord are always strong
> I am longing to discover
> Both the closeness and the awe
> Feel the nearness of your whisper
> Hear the glory of your roar
> Just knowing you, hearing you speak
> Seeing you move mysteriously
> Your whisperings in my soul's ear
> I want the friendship and the fear
> Of knowing you[16] **❞**
>
> **— Matt Redman**

O Nebuchadnezzar, we do not need to defend ourselves before you in this matter. If we are thrown into the blazing furnace, the God we serve is able to save us from it, and he will rescue us from your hand, O king. But even if he does not, we want you to know, O king, that we will not serve your gods or worship the image of gold you have set up (Da 3:16-18).

Sound doctrine teaches us how to fear the Lord. That's where wisdom starts.

Discipline: Ready, Set...

Elisabeth Elliot wrote a wonderful book entitled *Discipline, The Glad Surrender*. The title alone counters the common notion of spiritual disciplines as the busywork of the Christian life. Now, I don't want to add my voice to the guilt chorus that sings in your conscience whenever you think about your unmet spiritual-discipline goals. Nor will I discuss the strategies and benefits of the various spiritual disciplines. (The recommended books at the end of this study can assist you with that.) I want you to see how the practice of the spiritual disciplines, by increasing our wisdom, helps us make better decisions.

> **❝** The disciple is one who, intent upon becoming Christlike and so dwelling in his 'faith and practice,' systematically and progressively rearranges his affairs to that end.[17] **❞**
>
> — **Dallas Willard**

If you are a Christian making any effort in your walk in God, you are a disciple—you are engaged in spiritual disciplines. The issue is the quality and effectiveness of the disciplines you are employing (or neglecting). Jesus said "make disciples," not just converts. The Greek word translated "disciple" means "student followers." It speaks of enthusiastic apprentices who follow the master around, learning his ways by observing what he does and says.

That is one of the benefits of spiritual disciplines: they promote followership. As Donald Whitney keenly observes, "Learning and following involve discipline, for those who only *learn accidentally* and *follow incidentally* are not true disciples."[18] Have you ever met bumper-car believers—Christians who learn mostly by accident? The only time the course of their lives changes is when they get hit by something that sends them in a different direction. They want to change but they depend on random collisions to trigger growth in their lives.

People who live this way don't benefit much from their mistakes. The same errors keep coming back, and bad-habit ruts quickly become ditches. Why? Because these folks aren't prepared to change. When your life is spent going with the flow it's tough to change course in midstream. The Bible calls this folly, and folly does not sit at the same table with wisdom.

When I was growing up, there lived in my neighborhood a large dog named Tucky. When it came to chasing cars, Tucky had an unusual technique. Rather than run-

Meditate on Matthew 28:16-20. If you are a Christian, at what point in your life did you move from being a convert to being a disciple?

Meditate on Proverbs 6:9-11. Are there any areas in your life in which you act like a sluggard?

ning behind or alongside a vehicle in the traditional fashion, Tucky would run straight at the side of a moving car and ram the door with his head. This may have scared the wits out of many a driver, but it also took its toll on Tucky, especially his looks.

Now, Tucky had good intentions, for chasing cars was an honorable practice among the neighborhood dogs. But he was undisciplined in the chase, and his method lacked wisdom. Stuck in a bad habit, he never learned from his mistakes. One day, to everyone's dismay and no one's surprise, Tucky met his match against a well-armored pickup truck.

Don't be a Tucky. Be a disciple. Allow the spiritual disciplines to train you in wisdom and the ways of God. Over time you'll be better able to identify God's will in specific situations, and you'll be prepared to act accordingly.

The spiritual disciplines also open us up to the various means of God's grace and guidance. Have you ever vacationed at a cabin or beach house that had been closed up for quite some time? What is the first thing you do? Open a window, let some fresh air in! As you open windows and doors, the gentle breeze begins to flow through and the stuffiness dissipates.

Our lives can be like stuffy, closed-up houses. The spiritual disciplines act like open windows. And just like the cross-breezes that flow when windows are open, the various spiritual disciplines work together to allow a flow of grace through our lives. Bible study enriches our prayer. Fasting and solitude sharpen our listening. Service emboldens our evangelism. Over time the stuffy old house of our lives can begin to look more like a garden gazebo, with more openings than walls. The great thing about having a gazebo life is that, not only does the breeze blow through uninhibited, but there is clear vision all around.

---

4 We all have areas of our lives where we allow chaos to reign. In which of the following areas do you, through lack of discipline, give chaos the upper hand?

❏ Your car (including the trunk)

❏ Your dresser drawers

❏ Your bathroom

❏ Your briefcase or purse

❏ Your personal files and papers

In times of confusion and indecision, wouldn't you like to be able to say with the writer of Proverbs, "For wisdom will enter your heart, and knowledge will be pleasant to your soul" (Pr 2:10)? The spiritual disciplines are God's means of positioning us to hear his voice and respond to his guidance. They are wisdom at work on a daily basis.

Direction: Wisdom Applied

You can probably see where this study is heading. Our decision-making isn't so much about "finding God's will," as if it had gotten lost like socks in the laundry. God's will IS. Our goal is to flow along with it as cooperatively as possible, ever conscious of the fact that God does not guide us so we can better manage our own way, but so that we can go his way.

In regard to God's will, we may prefer to think of ourselves as intrepid explorers of divine mysteries, but we're a lot more like what Scripture calls us: sheep who need to be led and guided at every turn. He calls, he leads, and we follow. Wisdom is about learning to be led by the Good Shepherd when all our sheep-ness would have us wander elsewhere.

For Further Study:
Read 1 Kings 19:1-18. How did God present himself to Elijah? How do you assume God would reveal himself to you?

---

5 If Jesus is the Good Shepherd, we must be the sheep. Which of the following characteristics of sheep would you least like ascribed to you?

❏ They don't really do anything, they're only good for their wool

❏ They have no natural defenses

❏ They have no sense of direction

❏ Even when they are clean, they smell bad

In John 10:4, Jesus tells us there are two aspects to following: hearing the voice of the shepherd and following where the shepherd leads. Do you realize that we don't have to train our ears to hear the shepherd's voice? Jesus says we will know his voice when he speaks. From your first day as a Christian you were alive to the fact that God is in open, recognizable communication with you. It is one of the first things a new Christian notices.

Not only that, in our conversion we received the Holy

PERSONAL RETREATS

Did you ever have important decisions to make or heavy issues to sort out, but found yourself too busy or frazzled to think straight? I have found personal retreats to be a great way to clear my head and settle my heart. Each time I have taken a personal retreat I have come away with fresh perspective and faith, even if I didn't necessarily resolve any of the questions I was wrestling with. Here are some tips on how to approach a personal retreat.

There are many types of retreats. Most of the time you are getting away by yourself to spend time alone with God, but you can also use a retreat for personal planning, study, or evaluation.

If possible, an overnight retreat is best, but even a day away can be very beneficial.

Try to find a place that is restful and not too close or too far away. I try to get at least a half hour away but wouldn't want to drive more than two hours to get somewhere. Any place with televisions, computers, or lavish accommodations is not a good retreat location.

A retreat is an opportunity for rest. Most of us do not realize how tired we are or can become. So, first and foremost, let yourself stop and rest. This may or may not include additional sleep time. And remember, it takes time for our minds and bodies to slow down and for our hearts to settle. Be patient.

Don't bring a big agenda. The Lord knows what you need. Make it your prayer to enjoy his presence. Whether this be during rest, walks, or other ways, ask him to control the time and agenda, and respond to his prompting. God is very practical and we can trust him in the details.

Many people fast during retreats. While this is certainly not a requirement, I think food should be simple, the idea being that we want to give ourselves, our time, and our focus to other things.

Include worship in your time. If you play guitar, take one with you. Recorded worship music can also help.

Study materials are good, but the goal is NOT to knock out a backlog of reading or master a topic, but to encounter God through what you read. There are many devotional books that can be very helpful.

Bible study is essential, but again, the goal is not to find answers as much as to allow the Holy Spirit to illuminate God's Word in our hearts.

Take notes to reflect on later.

I have found that it is not uncommon for most of a personal retreat to be spent without any great experiences, but that there are moments of true communion with the Lord and even answers to prayer that come if we are patient.

Enjoy the process and leave the goals to God.

Spirit within us, a divine "guidance counselor" who helps us respond to the Good Shepherd (Jn 16:13-15). We actually have to train our ears *not* to hear his voice—through unbelief, worldliness, distraction, and the like. As Jack Deere has noted, "Although the voice of God runs through all experiences, most of us have diligently trained ourselves to ignore his voice and get on with the business of life."[19] This echoes Jesus' cryptic expression, "Let him who has ears, hear." Let's rediscover our spiritual ears.

> **“** Rather than looking for some sort of wrapped spiritual package from the Almighty, I want to rely upon my closeness to Him. So when I wonder about which job offer to take, I don't go through a divination process to discover the hidden message of God. Instead I examine how God has called me to live my life; what my motives are; what He has given me a heart for; where I am in my walk with Christ; and what God is saying to me through His word and His people.[20] **”**
>
> **— Bruce Waltke**

When we do listen for God, we find his communication is not typically information-oriented. Rather, he is directive. He communicates primarily to lead, not to explain. And when he does instruct, he gives us enough to obey, but not enough to figure him out. This troubles our modern minds, because we see the remaining elements of mystery as information unfairly withheld. But God holds out mystery as a promise of future revelation. Mystery is meant to draw out faith—the certainty of what we do not see (Heb 11:1). Remember, we're called to follow, not blaze our own trails. So as we turn our ears toward the shepherd's voice, and walk in the leading he gives us, we can have confidence that we are in the will of God.

Putting Wisdom Into Play

In concluding this study, I'd like to offer some practical tips for applying wisdom to our decisions.

Wise decisions flow out of godly convictions. When faced with an important decision, remember that our choices are not made in a vacuum. Our convictions—the sound doctrines that we can and should hold about God and his revealed will for our lives—provide a crucial perspective for the questions that confront us. Our convictions also allow us to plan ahead. If I am considering going to graduate school or buying a house, my convictions regarding my use of time, my priorities, finances, etc. will shape how I approach the decision. As long as I

For Further Study:
Read Philemon. Based on the information found in this letter,what are some of the convictions Paul held?

am walking in those convictions I can explore my options with confidence and creativity. "Many are the plans in a man's heart, but it is the LORD'S purpose that prevails" (Pr 19:21).

All convictions start with the great commandment. "Love the Lord your God with all your heart and with all your soul and with all your mind….and love your neighbor as yourself" (Mt 22:37-39). If our decisions are governed by these higher goals, they won't be dominated by our lesser desires like greed, ambition, pride, etc. Convictions are the fear of God at work in our lives.

Wise decisions are made in the environment of counsel. One key source of wisdom from God is plain old everyday advice. "Wisdom is found in those who take advice" (Pr 13:10). When you're faced with a major decision, do you habitually invite input from others? This can mean people close to you (friends, roommates, siblings), people who provide oversight in your life (pastors, parents, even bosses in some cases); people who are like you in temperament; people who look at things from a totally different perspective; people who have faced similar decisions; and people who generally exhibit godly wisdom in their lives. To seek advice is to walk in wisdom.

> **❝** The next best thing to being wise oneself is to live in a circle of those who are.[21] **❞**
> — **C.S. Lewis**

Let me note two things here. Getting advice doesn't mean letting others make decisions for you. And it doesn't mean that all the input you get from others must be consistent to be helpful. Get the necessary input, and take it before God.

Meditate on Proverbs 15:22. Make a list of the people you would go to for counsel in an important decision. Is this a well-rounded group?

It might seem that getting advice brings us wisdom because others have insight we lack. That's true, but it's only half the picture. When getting advice, God grants us wisdom because of the humility demonstrated by our willingness to draw others into our decisions. (By contrast, pride drives us to make isolated, impulsive, unilateral decisions that we come to regret.) "When pride comes, then comes disgrace, but with humility comes wisdom" (Pr 11:2). Don't yield to your pride. Seek advice.

Wise decisions are prayed through, not worried through. I was speaking one day with a woman trying to decide where to move. She listed a number of fears that had come to grip her, paralyzing her in the decision. Most of her mental effort was being expended, not in figuring out the details of the decision, but in warding off her anxi-

66

> **"** Prayer is the mightiest engine God has placed in our hands. It is the best weapon to use in every difficulty, and the surest remedy in every trouble. It is the key that unlocks the treasury of promises, and the hand that draws forth grace and help in time of need.[22] **"**
>
> — **J.C. Ryle**

For Further Study:
Read Philippians 4:4-9. What are some "to do's" from this passage that can help you battle anxiety?

ety over the situation. Her problem largely came down to her view of God (her theology), as expressed in a single worry: "Will God be there for me if I step out?" Corrie Ten Boom, a single woman who knew her share of challenging decisions, had this to say about worry: "Worry does not empty tomorrow of its sorrow, it empties today of its strength.... It is the interest you pay on trouble before it comes."[23] Paul's wonderful antidote to worry and anxiety in Philippians 4:6-7—thankful prayer— is more than good advice. If, when with faced a big decision, we would pray whenever we are tempted to worry, we would find ourselves not only with the peace "which transcends all understanding," but with a great deal more understanding as well.

Wise decisions require patience. When I was a young Christian, I was privileged to play guitar in my church's worship band. One day my guitar was irreparably damaged. Fearing I would lose my spot in the band, I borrowed some money, rushed out, and bought a new guitar. In my haste, I ended up paying too much for a guitar I didn't really like. It was a rash decision and I regretted it, as I have all the hasty decisions I have made. Had I been patient I would have made a better purchase *and* I would have seen God's provision at work, instead of my own impulsiveness. "A man's wisdom gives him patience" (Pr 19:10).

John Piper vividly describes the contrast between patience and impatience in seeking God's guidance.

> Impatience is a form of unbelief. It's what we begin to feel when we start to doubt the wisdom of God's timing or the goodness of God's guidance....[Patience is] a deepening, ripening, peaceful willingness to wait for God in the unplanned place of obedience, and to walk with God at the unplanned pace of obedience—to wait in his place, and go at his pace.[24]

Prior to making a big decision, many Christians take time away in a spiritual retreat. This serves as a forced shut-down of our impatience factory, allowing us to "wait in his place, and go at his pace." Wisdom is best cultivated in a climate of patience.

6 Briefly describe your ideal environment for a personal spiritual retreat.

Wise decisions are not risk-proof. Eventually, after all the preparation, evaluation, and prayer, we still need to act. All wise decisions need decisiveness. Indecision and procrastination are never wise. It is rare, before making a decision, to have neat and tidy answers to all our questions. Typically, we must launch the ship not knowing exactly how well it will float. At these times, we find our ultimate peace in knowing that God has not created us for infallibility. Wisdom is not risk-free living; there is no such thing.

> **" We may insist on God telling us what to do because we live in fear or are obsessed with *being right* as a strategy for *being safe*.** [25]
>
> **— Dallas Willard**

Thus, we may at times make decisions that do not turn out as we would have wanted or hoped. Does this mean we somehow have messed up God's will for our lives? Has our error caused God's cosmic hard drive to crash? By no means! Jerry Bridges notes, "We do have a responsibility to make wise decisions...But God's plan for us is not contingent upon our decisions. God's plan is not contingent at all. God's plan is sovereign. It includes our foolish decisions as well as our wise ones." [26]

Our confidence rests in two truths. The first is that, to God, *the decisions we make are no more important than the process by which we make them*. God has no problem putting us where he wants us. Scripture tells of God moving people around in the craziest ways—in great big arks and little reed baskets, in chariots of fire and bellies of big fish. It's God's job to put you in the right place at the right time. He glories in orchestrating the course of our lives.

The primary reason God gives us decisions to make is that he wants to do something *in* us, not just with us.

For Further Study:
Read Colossians 1:9-12. What results does Paul seek as he prays for the Colossians?

Decisions and mysteries are God's invitation to trust him. God uses our personal crises as opportunities for us to grow closer to him. Almost every decision we make can be undone, but the process by which we make decisions settles into our lives as habit, producing consistent results either good or bad, depending on the wisdom brought to the process. God is at work within us and uses the *process* of decision-making to form his character and will in our lives.

Romans 8:28 is a wonderful promise for Christians faced with big decisions: "In all things God works for the good of those who love him, who have been called according to his purpose." All things?! Even my decisions that didn't turn out as I'd expected? Even my honest mistakes? You bet. "All things" doesn't leave much room for us to mess up God's agenda.

My computer has a recycle bin where all the "permanent changes" to my documents go. Because of that bin, I don't have to worry about deleting files by mistake. I have confidence to make file-related decisions. Romans 8:28 is kind of like the recycle bin of the Bible. Because of this promise, we can make decisions to the best of our ability and leave the results to God. And God will take those decisions and make them work—for his glory and our good.

So if you regret a decision made in the past, trust God that he will recycle it into a good thing for you. Prepare yourself for a life of wisdom through sound doctrine and spiritual disciplines. If you are living today in the valley of indecision, listen for the voice of the Good Shepherd, and follow where he leads. Don't be afraid of decisions. Ask for what you lack. Ask for wisdom. And the promise of Proverbs 2:1-10 will be your supply:

> My son, if you accept my words and store up my commands within you, turning your ear to wisdom and applying your heart to understanding, and if you call out for insight and cry aloud for understanding, and if you look for it as for silver and search for it as for hidden treasure, then you will understand the fear of the LORD and find the knowledge of God. For the LORD gives wisdom, and from his mouth come knowledge and understanding. He holds victory in store for the upright, he is a shield to those whose walk is blameless, for he guards the course of the just and protects the way of his faithful ones. Then you will understand what is right and just and fair— every good path. For wisdom will enter your heart, and knowledge will be pleasant to your soul. ∎

1. Describe a good decision you have made and how you made it.

2. What are some decisions single people make that married people don't have to think about?

3. Think of the wisest person you've known. How did he or she exhibit wisdom?

4. Name some kinds of motives can complicate our decisions.

Answers to Warm-up
(from page 53)

René Descartes: "I think, therefore I am."

Sören Kierkegaard: "Truth is subjectivity."

Karl Marx: "Religion is the opiate of the people."

Jean Paul Sartre: "Man is condemned to be free."

How do these classic examples of man's wisdom stack up against the wisdom of Scripture?

5. Describe the last time you had a debate with someone about doctrine. What was it about? What did you learn? What would you say or do differently if you had that debate again today?

6. What spiritual discipline would you most like to develop, and why?

7. What is the greatest hindrance you face to being aware of God's leading?

8. What are three convictions that you want to base your decisions on?

9. If you wanted to draw from the counsel of another person, who would you go to first, and why?

10. What are some signs that someone is struggling with anxiety? (See page 14)

11. Describe a time when you stepped out in faith and experienced the timely help of God.

RECOMMENDED READING

Spiritual Disciplines for the Christian Life by Donald S. Whitney (Colorado Springs, CO: NavPress, 1991)

A Call to Spiritual Reformation by D.A. Carson (Grand Rapids, MI: Baker Book House, 1992)

Discovering God's Will by Sinclair B. Ferguson (Carlisle, PA: Banner of Truth, 1982)

Disciplined for Life by John Loftness and C.J. Mahaney (Gaithersburg, MD: PDI Communications, 1992)

RICH IN IMPACT

Strategy: The rich single life resonates with the impact of a whole-hearted devotion to God and his agenda for our lives.

BIBLE STUDY 2 Corinthians 4:7

WARM-UP Marni Nixon had a brush with fame for which of the following reasons?

1. She sang with Amy Grant in a duo called "The Gospel Songbirds" before Amy made it big as a solo artist.
2. The niece of former president Richard Nixon, she was once engaged to Conrad Kennedy of the Massachusetts Kennedy clan.
3. She was the real female lead singing voice for some of the major movie musicals in Hollywood history.
4. She is the diminutive British actress who performed in the costume of C3PO in the first three *Star Wars* movies.

(See page 88 for answer)

PERSONAL STUDY The bit players of the Bible fascinate me—those people who show up for a few verses and then disappear, never to be mentioned again. I think of Simeon and Anna waiting patiently for the coming of the Messiah. I think of Zacchaeus, the tree-climbing tax collector. What ever happened to this radical guy? Or Dorcas, the gracious woman whom Paul raised from the dead. How did that miracle change her life?

One of the most intriguing biblical bit players is Demas. Demas is mentioned briefly by Paul in three of his letters. He was evidently a Greek convert to Christianity and traveled with Paul on his journeys. He apparently stayed close to Paul during his first imprisonment; Paul's prison letters to Philemon and the Colossians both mention Demas by name. We know that Paul considered Demas a "fellow worker" (Phm 24), among the highest tributes Paul could pay to those who served with him. Demas was apparently dear to Paul. He stayed with him in dark times, bringing him the refreshment of friendship. Demas worked and sacrificed for the cause.

But the last word on Demas is not a good one. In prison and awaiting death, Paul closes his last letter to Timothy lamenting that many had left him. He says of Demas, "because he loved this world, [he] has deserted me" (2Ti 4:10). Think about this for a second. A man who worked with Paul for almost Paul's entire ministry, who had labored in the founding of churches, and who made his stand at Paul's first arrest, suddenly turns his back on the dear old servant of God and walks away. After all the trials he must have endured at Paul's side, what could have been so powerful to harden the heart of the once-faithful Demas?

Meditate on Philippians 2:19-30. Reflect on the differences between Demas and Epaphroditus.

Paul's reason is cryptically succinct. Demas "loved this world." Persecution, hardship, and imprisonment had forged a friendship, but in the end Paul's "fellow worker" was undone by love of the world. Demas the good soldier became forever known as Demas the deserter. What is this "love of the world" that could so damage a person's spiritual destiny?

Do Not Love the World

The Apostle John gives us a crystal-clear view of what it means to love the world. In addressing those who would find themselves in the valley of a Demas decision, John cautions:

> Do not love the world or anything in the world. If anyone loves the world, the love of the Father is not in him. For everything in the world—the cravings of sinful man, the lust of his eyes and the boasting of what he has and does—comes not from the Father but from the world. The world and its desires pass away, but the man who does the will of God lives forever (1Jn 2:15-17).

The "world" John describes here is not the world that "God so loved" (Jn 3:16)—referring to people in need of the Savior. The "world" John warns us against has been described by one commentator as "the organized system of human civilization which is opposed to God and alienated from God." It is human existence without reference

For Further Study:
Read Luke 4:1-13.
What temptations of
the world did Satan
offer Jesus in the
wilderness?

to God, existence as if eternity did not matter. This world—infested as it is with idolatry, cravings, and boastings, a world that captures hearts and destroys lives—is all anyone can know apart from Christ. It is the love of this world that brought down Demas.

For the Christian single in our day, the "world" and its temptations can take many forms. R.C. Sproul graphically describes the challenge of the Christian in the world:

> We live in this world. We are part of the world. We are to a certain degree products of this world. And the world is our battlefield....The world is a seducer. It seeks to attract our attention and our devotion. It remains so close at hand, so visible, so enticing. It eclipses our view of heaven....It pleases us—much of the time anyway—and, alas, we often live our lives to please it. And that is where conflict ensues, for pleasing the world so seldom overlaps with pleasing God.[1]

Consider, for example, the temptations found in advertisements. It is estimated that you and I are exposed to about 3,000 advertisements per day, on average roughly one every 20 seconds of our waking lives.[2] Most of these ads seek to appeal to some basic desire—to possess, experience, control, consume, avoid—all of which beckon us to worldliness. Every day, we face the unrelenting assault of such enticements.

> **❝** Materialism will inevitably produce the kind of society....where people know the price of everything, but the value of nothing—where people have a great deal to live on, but very little to live for.[3] **❞**
> — **Randy Alcorn**

Out of millions of Internet sites to choose from, sites devoted to pornography consistently hold several of the top five slots—an alarming testimony to the insatiable sexual lusts and cravings in our culture. Religion itself can be worldly. Deepak Chopra, guru of the 1990s, once described his appeal this way: "They say you have to give up everything to be spiritual, get away from the world, all that junk. I satisfy a spiritual yearning without making [people] think they have to worry about God."[4] When we crave attention, lust after position, or boast of our achievements, we are demonstrating love of the world. In short, worldliness seeks to—and is fully able to—infect every level of our lives.

The Bible teaches that we live in a world that "hates" the things of God (Jn 15:18), that will give us much trou-

For Further Study:
Read Romans 1:18-25.
How can we have an
awareness of God yet
insist on living as if he
doesn't matter?

ble (Jn 16:33), that is hollow and deceptive (Col 2:8), that will be like pollution to our souls (Jas 1:27), and that will eventually pass away (1Co 7:31). We are told not to be conformed to the world (Ro 12:2) and to flee from the world (1Ti 6:11). Yet Jesus prayed for us this way, "My prayer is not that you take them out of the world but that you protect them from the evil one....As you sent me into the world, I have sent them into the world" (Jn 17:15, 18).

Historically, Christians have had two basic tendencies when dealing with the world. One is to withdraw, avoiding worldly influences as much as possible. The other is to conform, trying to be as much like the world as possible. Perhaps you have found yourself caught up in one of these extremes. Early in this century Oswald Chambers wrote about the challenge of being "in the world but not of it."[6] He addressed the need for Christians to avoid such extremes, neither living in fearful withdrawal from the world, nor being indistinguishable from it. Chambers was talking about how to live in a fallen world *for* Christ because you have been placed here *by* Christ.

Meditate on 1 Kings 11:1-13. Why do you think Solomon's great wisdom did not protect him from this sad end?

1 Which of these activities would be considered worldly in your Christian circles? Why not search the Scriptures to double-check your convictions in these areas?

❏ Flirting

❏ Having NFL season tickets

❏ Reading *People* magazine

❏ Hunting

❏ Drinking alcohol socially

❏ Voting Democratic

❏ Having friends who are homosexual

❏ Surfing the Internet

❏ Watching R-rated movies

❏ Investing in the stock market

❏ Not hunting

❏ Listening to non-Christian radio

❏ Watching PG-13 movies

How do you relate to the world? Do you try to hide from it? Would people have trouble distinguishing in your life where the world ends and your faith begins? Do you long to find ways to bring the truth of liberty in Christ into collision with the enslaving ways of the world? Do you want to influence your corner of this fallen world for Christ with your singleness? Let's take the rest of this study to explore some ways that you as a single adult can meet that challenge, and make a difference that will change the lives of others.

An Agenda for Lasting Impact

I began taking guitar lessons when I was in third grade. From my earliest memories of playing guitar, I wanted to be a rock star. Through my high-school years it was my consuming fantasy. I went to every concert I could, studying the posturing and moves of my idols— Clapton, Springsteen, Pete Townsend, Keith Richards. I never practiced enough to actually play really well, but I knew how to look cool on a stage!

My big break finally came in college, when I got involved in a band with some other dreamers. At our first concert, hundreds of rowdy students jammed into a little coffeehouse to hear us. The show was great! Three hours of classic-rock cover tunes, all my favorites. We were all over the stage, jumping into the crowd—some of our equipment even caught on fire! It all culminated in a raucous, unrehearsed finale of "Summertime Blues." At the end of the show I stood on the stage, holding my guitar in triumphal, heroic glee, eating up the glory as fellow students screamed out my name. At age 20 I had achieved my life's dream. It was seriously cool.

The downside hit me a short time later. Like about an hour later. Sitting on my bed back in my dorm room, it began to sink in: "I'm 20 years old and I have just accomplished the only thing that ever mattered to me. The rest of my life is going to be a real bummer." That was seriously uncool.

What is your life dream? What is your view of success? How will you know when you have finally "made it" in life?

We must have goals beyond success. We live in a goal-driven, success-obsessed culture. In this affluent society, most of us can set our sights on a dream and have reasonable expectations of obtaining it. To succeed in your

For Further Study:
Read Genesis 24. What was the definition of success that Abraham's servant desired?

For Further Study:
Read 1 Samuel 13:1-15. How did impatience rob Saul of his future?

Meditate on Hebrews 11:31-40. When will these saints receive the full benefit of their success?

career, outwork the competition. To attain a certain standard of living, just borrow your way there. Within the limits of our natural abilities, we can pursue almost any kind of success we want. But two critical questions often go unanswered in our full-throttle chase after dreams. Will the pursuit of success satisfy us? And, will it allow us to leave a meaningful mark on our world?

This question took on fresh relevance for me when I became a pastor. I entered the ministry at a time when it seemed like every other week some well-known religious leader was being exposed as a fraud or confessing major sin. I began to wonder if I would be able to resist the temptations and pressures that had snared these men. I certainly was no better than they were. More than anything, I wanted to carry out my ministry well until the end of my days. But I was gripped by a deep fear that, somewhere along the line, serious moral failure would be inevitable.

As I examined this fear before the Lord, he began to encourage me by his Spirit. He reminded me that if I kept my attention on him, he would preserve my call. But he also gave me some fatherly advice. As I was driving to work one day pondering my future, I sensed him speak to my heart, "My son, people who finish well are people who have goals beyond success."

Meditate on Acts 9:1-19. How was Paul's vision of success changed?

The apostle Paul had an interesting perspective on success. He was among the social elite of his day—not just a good Jew, but "a Hebrew of Hebrews" (Php 3:5), and prominent among the movers and shakers in Israel. But a funny thing happened on a business trip. A dramatic encounter with the risen Christ on the Damascus Road created a major pile-up on Paul's highway to success. That encounter with Christ redefined Paul's goals.

Fast-forward several years. Paul sits alone in a prison cell. The sentence of death may draw the curtain of his life closed at any moment. On some grimy parchment he scratches out his thoughts:

> **❝** If you are God-centered, you will adjust your circumstances to what God wants to do. God has a right to interrupt your life. He is Lord. When you surrendered to Him as Lord, you gave Him the right to help Himself to your life anytime He wants.[7] **❞**
>
> — **Henry Blackaby, Claude King**

To Timothy, my dear son....You know that everyone in the province of Asia has deserted me....For I am already being poured out like a drink offering, and the time has come for my departure....At my first defense, no one came to my support, but everyone deserted me. May it not be held against them. But the Lord stood at my side and gave me strength (2Ti 1:2,15; 4:6,16-17).

Was Paul a success? By whose definition? If you think of him as a man who was given the best of everything in the society of his day, he was a testimony to wasted potential. If you think of him as a gifted preacher who spent many of his best years in prison unable to use the gifts God had given him, his life was a tragedy of missed opportunity. But Paul's personal inventory tells a different story: "I have fought the good fight, I have finished the race, I have kept the faith. Now there is in store for me the crown of righteousness, which the Lord, the righteous Judge, will award to me on that day" (2Ti 4:7-8).

Did Paul regret the work left undone? Probably. Was he perplexed that many of the people into whom he had poured his life had turned against him? Certainly. Would Paul have rather spent his final days in more comfortable surroundings? Wouldn't you? Did Paul consider himself a failure? Absolutely not.

Paul understood that although success is fine, the highest goal in the Christian life is faithfulness. Mother Theresa, who in her life set an impressive, decades-long example of service to the poorest of the poor, was once asked if she ever became discouraged in her service. She replied, "No, because Jesus called us to be faithful, not successful."[8]

For Further Study:
Read 2 Corinthians 12:1-10. What did Paul choose to boast in? Why?

> 66 In any Christian view of life, self-fulfillment must never be permitted to become the controlling issue. The issue is service, the service of real people. The question is, 'How can I be most useful?', not, 'How can I feel most useful?'[9]
>
> — D.A. Carson

Success is a temporary, peak experience, not a lifestyle. And success is relative: anyone can succeed if allowed to set the standard himself. In God's eyes, the height of our success is far less significant than the consistency of our faithfulness. Where worldly success is about achievement and conquest, biblical success is about who we are and how we finish our race. The beautiful thing about biblical success is that, in our pursuit of it, all of heaven's resources are at our disposal. If you want to have an impact as a single person, it's fine to enjoy earthly success, but set your goals beyond success—be faithful, and finish well.

2 Which of the following would you consider the most rewarding honor for yourself? Why?

❏ An Olympic Gold Medal   ❏ A Nobel Prize

❏ An Oscar   ❏ The Medal of Honor

❏ A Gold Record

What we are a part of is more important than the part we play. Here are two comments representative of many I've heard from single women and men over the years.

Comment #1: "The vice president of the company says they see me as having great potential. If I can give them three years on the fast track, I can write my ticket anywhere. It's a lot of travel, but I figure it will pay off in all I can do for God when I'm done."

Comment #2: "It seems like every time I sing my songs, people respond. Everybody says I should make a record so more people can hear my music, but I'd have to move to Nashville to do it. That's just the way the business is. But if I have a gift, shouldn't I find out what my potential is?"

> ❝ May the Lord, in mercy to my soul, save me from setting up an idol of any sort in His room, as I do by preferring a work professedly for Him to communion with Him.[10] ❞
>
> — **Henry Martyn,**
> **19th century missionary**
> **and life-long single man**

Both of these issues, and countless others like them, address a larger question: "How do I use the gifts and talents God has given me?" What counsel would you give in the situations described above? I generally respond with what may seem like an odd question: *"Why do you feel you need to reach your potential?"* This is a question that may challenge every lesson you have ever been taught. How would you answer it?

Let's examine the Bible's perspective on that question. First, Scripture says very little about using our gifts to their fullest potential. When Paul talks about spiritual gifts (in 1 Corinthians 12, for example), he is not encouraging folks to "find your gift." He is not recommending a gifts seminar or a spiritual-gifts evaluation test. He sees gifts spilling out all over the place and is calling people to use their gifts in an orderly and humble manner.

Paul describes the spiritual gifts as parts of a body. He

**Meditate on Romans
12:3-8.** What guidance
does this passage offer
for maintaining humility
in the context of fully
expressing our gifts?

does not say to the hand, "You need to reach your fullest
potential as a hand," nor to the eye, "You know what's
holding you back from really being something special? It's
these two unreliable ears next to you." When people view
the body, Paul wants them to see all the parts working
"for the common good" (1Co 12:7)—a body working like a
body should. While we *are* encouraged to "eagerly desire
the greater gifts" (1Co 12:30) and "fan into flame the
gifts" (2Ti 1:6) the larger issue is, "Why? To what end are
we to pursue these gifts?"

On this point, the Bible is quite clear. *The use of our
gifts is never intended for our personal fulfillment.
Rather, it is always for the building up of the church, the
body of Christ*. From this it follows that our gifts and call-
ings have no real value apart from their contribution to
the body, the church of Christ, and its mission in the
world.

If you're like me, you first became a Christian, then
you started going to church, because everyone knows
good Christians go to church. That's American
Christianity 101. The reality, however, is we are saved *into*
the body of Christ. We don't go to church, we *are* the
church! The church is not some cosmic concept, some
heavenly fraternity we sometimes kind of feel around us;
it is the people of God, set apart for his purposes.

When it comes to the church, Christians are not, and
can never be, "believers but not belongers." The Church
Universal, the Bride of Christ, expresses itself at the level
of daily life in individual local congregations. From the
very beginning (see Acts 2) Scripture has directed every
member of the universal church to be an active partici-
pant in a *local* church. This local community of faith
includes not only dear old Pastor Bob and Wanda the
Angelic-Voiced Worshiper, but Ed the Obnoxious Zealot
and Betty the Chronic Whiner as well. Oh yes, you and I
also bring our little casserole of mixed motives and limited skills to the party. Believe it or not, the imperfect
church is the place God hangs out, it is the thing God says
he will build, and it is the humble vessel through which
he will reach the world.

For Further Study:
Read Acts 2:37-47.
God used the preaching
of Peter to establish
the first local church.
What characteristics of
that church does
Scripture highlight?

How can we have an impact in the cramped confines of
a local church? Jesus told his disciples, "Whoever wants to
become great among you must be your servant" (Mt
20:26). The Lord, by the way, backed this principle up with
his very life. Where the world says "Be all you can be,"
Jesus says, "He who loses his life for my sake will find it"
(Mt 16:24). The door to fulfillment of our call, expression

of our gifts, and lasting impact in the world is opened by one key: the key of servanthood. As a single adult, you have a precious opportunity to make an impact on this world, but that opportunity begins through serving in the context of a local church, God's tangible presence in the world.

---

3 What spiritual gift or gifts do you presently desire? Write down three, and a brief reason why you desire these particular gifts.

•

•

•

Reason:

Joshua Harris is a young single guy I know. He has many gifts and talents and has made quite a mark in publishing a national magazine, writing a best-selling book, and holding conferences across the country. Josh would be a first-round draft pick of any ministry organization. But he has gotten off the calling track. Josh has traded in his desire to be in ministry for a passion for serving in the local church. As he tells it:

> Too many people my age have lost a vision for the church....My dream is to be a part of bringing the church back to the place God has always meant for it to play in our lives....Someday I hope to pastor a church or serve under another man in whatever position I'm best suited for. I don't know all that the future holds, but I want to be in on the action, and I believe the action is in the local church.[12]

> **"** Adults who happen to be single are not more important than any other group in the church, but they are as important. They are not in a 'hallway' unto marriage but in a 'living' room full of potential and possibilities, which may or may not have an entrance leading to marriage but has many doors that lead to ministry.[11] **"**
>
> **— William White**

Do you suppose Josh might be right? That, as Scripture testifies, the action really is in the church?

When I focus on fulfilling my individual gifts and call-

Meditate on Hebrews 13:17. What is your attitude toward the leaders God has placed over you for your benefit in the church?

ing *as an individual*, my impact will be limited both by my gifts and my opportunities to use them. But taking a servanthood approach to fulfillment means throwing my gifts in with those of others in the church and seeing *the whole body in action*. This is impact multiplied. Then position, influence, recognition, ambition, and other idols of the world are far less likely to ensnare me, because I'm making my contribution with no strings attached.

Whether leading the parade or being "a doorkeeper in the house of God" (Ps 84:10), what we are a part of, as someone once noted, is more important than the part we play.

Know your assets and how to use them. Nick was a talented guy who managed the assets of investors by trading on the global stock market. He became a wheeler-dealer in a high-risk segment of the market, but he didn't really know the importance to his employer of the assets he was managing. To him, the assets were merely one of the components allowing him to play an exciting game.

> ❝ You don't have to have a college degree to serve. You don't have to make your subject and your verb agree to serve. You don't have to know about Plato and Aristotle to serve....You only need a heart full of grace. A soul generated by love.[13] ❞
>
> — **Martin Luther King**

Unfortunately, he didn't count on an earthquake in Japan destabilizing his market. He tried to adjust, but he was a gambler, and the only thing a gambler does well is gamble. By the time he gave up gambling he had lost some serious change—like about a billion dollars. His little mismanagement fiasco destroyed a 300-year-old bank, the bank that had once held the first mortgage on the Louisiana Purchase. Oops.

Nicholas Leeson never really understood the value or purpose of the assets that had been entrusted to him. What can we learn from Nick's debacle? First, don't get so caught up in what you're doing that you lose sight of why you're doing it. And second, you can squander your assets if you don't understand and use them well.

For Further Study: Read Luke 12:13-21. In what ways was the man in this parable foolish?

What do I mean by assets? Simply, those parts of our life and situation that we can choose to use for God's glory—or for other things. Every season of life provides certain assets. When I was four years old my assets were adorableness (so my mother says) and the fact that I didn't take up a lot of space in the family car. As a teenager my assets were plenty of energy and...well, that's probably it. Do you see the assets in your life that come from your singleness? Equally important, do you understand them and use them wisely?

USING OUR GIFTS

Steve Camp is a Christian musician with a long career in music ministry. As a well-known artist he has been around highly gifted people for many years. He recently issued a challenge to his fellow musicians who might be tempted to compromise God's best for the sake of worldly success in the recording industry. His challenge is in the form of a poster entitled "A Call for Reformation in the Contemporary Christian Music Industry." This call consists of 107 "theses" modeled on the 95 Theses of Martin Luther, which touched off the Protestant Reformation.

While not many of us have great artistic gifts, we all have gifts (1Co 12:7) for which we are responsible. Some of Camp's 107 challenges are applicable to anyone having a desire to make an impact in our world. Ponder the following excerpts from several of Steve Camp's theses.

#12: We fail to glorify God when we strive to please men rather than please God. (Gal 1:10; 1Th 2:4)

#62: Godly character exhibited in response to sound doctrine is paramount in serving the Lord. To live privately what we proclaim publicly is the manifestation of genuine faith. That is why from the stockroom to the stage Christ-likeness should evidence our behavior. God has not called us to be successful, but faithful. (2Co 6:3-10)

#64: Ministry is defined as service to God and his creatures as we employ our Spirit-given giftedness, according to the instruction of the Scripture as good stewards of the manifold grace of God for the advancement of his kingdom. (1Pe 4:10-12)

#65: God has designed genuine ministry to be inseparable from the life and leadership of the local church. Any ministry that does not strengthen one's commitment to the local church is inconsistent with the purposes of Christ. (Ac 2:42-47; Heb 10:23-25)

#84: We are not, however, called to isolationism. We are called to be salt and light in the world. We are to be faithful witnesses of God's mercy, love, and grace to the lost and dying. We are to cultivate personal relationships with unbelievers, love our neighbor and our enemy, serve them, and share our faith with them. (Mt 5:13-16; 40-44)

#92: To have a good name in the community-at-large is vital in representing Christ. We must demonstrate honest, equitable handling of the lesser things: business, money, trade, etc., in order to be entrusted with the superior things: His Word, the church, and the souls of men. (Ps 15:2-5; 1Ti 2:1-2; Tit 3:1-2)

#96: We will purpose to keep personal relationships more important than business deals; family more valuable than commodities; and faith more precious than fortune. The struggle is maintaining an eternal perspective in the transitory moments. May our light so shine before men. (Ps 90:12; Mt 5:16; Eph 5:22-23; Php 2:1-5; 1Pe 3:7)

I believe the most overlooked asset of singleness is flexibility. The average single adult has available to him or her a wonderful mix of time, energy, and resources with which to build a lifestyle overflowing with ministry impact and spiritual growth. Yet so often the choices made by singles rob them of this valuable gift of flexibility. How do we maximize our flexibility?

One key aspect of flexibility is time. A single woman once characterized her singleness as "drowning in time." Have you felt this way? The single life can seem heavy on time, and ways to randomly fill that time are expanding daily. How can our free time become "impact time"? Leland Ryken advises us well: "Time is the arena within which all human quests run their course. It is within time that the issues of life are contested and sometimes resolved. Without making one's peace with time, a person will not solve the question of how to find the good life."[14]

How do we "make our peace with time?" Do you steward your time, including your free time, or do you let outside influences determine how you use it? I am a slacker by temperament, but I've learned to schedule my time so that my slacker tendencies don't eat my life whole. My objective in time management is not to get as much done as possible, but to try to make sure that I end up doing what is best for me to do.

Meditate on Ephesians 5:15-16.
Are there any ways that you can make better use of your time?

For example, I tend to over-commit my evenings. So, I schedule every one, even if it is simply a "reading night" or an "off night." Then if something comes up, I have some options on how to handle it—it doesn't just infect my schedule like the flu, throwing off everything else in my life until I can regroup. I've also come to recognize how I can blow time (like in front of the tube), so I make a special effort to discipline myself in those areas.

---

4 Suppose your work or school gave you your birthday off. Whatever you want to do for eight hours, it's paid for! What would you do with your day?

I encourage the single folks I know to take regular overnight personal retreats—to break from the routine, be before the Lord, and just assess life. Let me encourage you to do the same. Use those times to set goals for progress, not perfection. Study the scriptural principle of the Sabbath, then apply what you learn. If you do things like this, will every moment become an impact moment? No. But impact will likely emerge "all by itself" from the ordered use of the time you do have.

Your flexibility will also be affected by your approach to work. As a single adult you are highly prized in the employment world for the sheer number of hours that can be sucked out of your life for the sake of the bottom line. Money, perks, travel, "opportunity," and promotions are all used as lures to get single folks to carry the time load no one else seems to want. Don't bite. This is the hook of the world lurking under the bait of career. Whether you work for yourself or for someone else, don't let career or job define you. Work hard, but work as unto the Lord. God is your boss, and in the end his advancement plan is the only one that counts.

> ❝ This is the only measure of our application to any worldly business…it must have no more of our hands, our hearts, or our time, than is consistent with a hearty, daily, careful preparation of ourselves for another life.[15] ❞
>
> — **William Law**

Another potential snare is possessions. I knew a Christian single woman who always seemed to be moving from one place to another. Was she an irritable person, unpleasant, hard to live with? No, she just had too much stuff. She always needed a large area in which to store her accumulated possessions, most of which weren't in use and could have easily been replaced if needed. But she had a false sense of security in her possessions. Her stuff had become her treasure, and in a sense she worshiped it. She passed up some great living opportunities because she thought it more important to protect her stuff than to be available for the adventure of God's purpose. As Jesus said, "Where your treasure is, there your heart will be also" (Mt 6:21).

The less stuff (car, house, music collections, etc.) we have to manage, the less chance our heart will attach to it, and the greater will be our flexibility for God's purpose. I'm not saying "stuff" is inherently bad, but we must recognize that our sinful nature will always tempt us to worship it.

Meditate on 2 Thessalonians 3:6-15. How does this passage speak to you about your employment goals?

84

5 You are anonymously given $100,000 (tax free, of course). The only requirements are that you may not invest or save any of it, and you must use it in six different ways. What would you do with your money?

1. _____

2. _____

3. _____

4. _____

5. _____

6. _____

One of my joys in pastoring single adults is learning second-hand how well they manage their asset of flexibility. I love to hear, "Did you know that so and so..." followed by a testimony, for example, of how some single brothers spent all morning shoveling snow from the walkways and driveways of single sisters in the church. Or how a group of single women have opened their home to anyone in the church who needs a place to hang out on a Sunday afternoon. These are just a couple of the ways single men and women in our church have learned to creatively manage the assets of their singleness for real impact. If only Nick Leeson had understood his assets and managed them with the same care.

Nothing reaches people like the aroma of the presence of God in our lives. I used to live in a house with many international students. Most of us were Christians, but we often had people living with us who were totally ignorant of Christianity. Keiko, a young Japanese woman, was among them. Keiko had never heard of Christ. She was in the United States alone, and knew no one but the folks in our house. She understood very little English and rarely had any meaningful conversation with the rest of us in the house.

Keiko thought all Americans were Christians. That was not good, because her experience with Americans was anything but Christian. "Christians" who had promised to house her if she came to the States never followed through. She had taken a job working for a "Christian," only to be harassed and eventually let go without pay. To top it all off, a woman who cleaned our house and claimed to be a Christian robbed her of the little money she had left. If anyone had reason to reject Christianity, it was Keiko.

Imagine my shock when she came up to me one day and announced in second-language English, "I have asked Jesus into my heart." I was blown away. "You can't," I thought, "I haven't told you how!" There was no earthly reason why she should have come to Christ. The only witness she had experienced taught her the opposite of what Christianity was about. I knew from her blank expressions during our house Bible studies that she hadn't gotten any usable information from us. Yet here she stood, clearly a changed woman. My desire to hear her story was not so much to rejoice with her as it was to figure out the mystery.

"Many people tell me they are Christian, they want to tell me about Jesus," she whispered through tears. "But here I meet Jesus, in you and your friends. I want people to meet him in me."

> **"** Why singleness? That the works of God might be made manifest in the deepest recesses of our beings. To declare God's glory in a fallen world. To show that God is enough for the human heart. To demonstrate to earth and hell the triumph of the life of God in the soul of man.[16] **"**
> — **Margaret Clarkson**

Meditate on 2 Corinthians 5:17-19. Are the people around you aware of God's appeal to them through your life?

6 Which of the following are NOT ways that God expresses himself through us to others?

- ☐ Light
- ☐ Report Card
- ☐ Letter
- ☐ Fragrance

For Further Study: Read Ephesians 2:4-10. What is it that God desires to display through us to others?

The Scriptures tell us that we are letters from Christ, written with the Spirit of the Living God on the tablets of our hearts (2Co 3:3-4). What a wonderful, encouraging picture! We don't simply deliver the message, somehow the message is printed in us for others to read. Paul describes us as the "aroma of Christ" (2Co 2:15) and as "jars of clay" (2Co 4:7) carrying the treasure of Christ. How many times I get discouraged at my lack of motivation to serve, at my flirtatious friendship with the world, at the reality that my witness is more often bland than bold. Yet daily I am reminded that it is God at work in me and through me that matters. He is the vine, I am the branch. My job is to bear fruit, not to start my own little orchard.

Does this mean I just "let go and let God?" How could I? If God wants to work through me, I want to do all I can to cooperate with the process. Do I need to root out some worldly weeds? Get me a backhoe and I'll dig up the whole field. Do I need to develop my tools? Teach me how. But mostly I want to draw close to my Jesus, to be more like him, to let his light be my light. I want the aroma of the smoke from God's fiery presence to envelop me. I want to smell like Jesus.

Charles Spurgeon once said, "He lives most and lives best who is the means of imparting spiritual life to others."[18] We are the means, Jesus is the life. Let your single life be one rich in impact—a full life poured out in Christ, by Christ, and for Christ. ■

GROUP DISCUSSION   1. In what ways can worldliness creep into the lives of Christians?

2. What challenges have you faced trying to be "in the world, but not of it"?

3. Describe a time you achieved something you had been dreaming about or working hard for. What was the feeling like? How do you view that achievement today?

4. In your line of work, what is the definition of success? What would you have to sacrifice to obtain it?

5. What spiritual gift do you desire? Why do you desire this gift?

6. Describe a time when you experienced Christians functioning well as a body.

7. What is the greatest current limitation (besides work or school) on your complete flexibility to serve the Lord?

8. What possession in your life would be most difficult to part with, and why?

9. Think of a person who to you most reflects the love of Christ. What is it about his or her life that you find most inspiring?

RECOMMENDED READING

Money, Possessions, and Eternity by Randy Alcorn (Wheaton, IL: Tyndale House Publishers, 1989)

Experiencing God by Henry Blackaby and Claude King (Broadman & Holman Publishers, 1994)

Pleasing God by R.C. Sproul (Wheaton, IL: Tyndale House Publishers, 1988)

ANSWER to Warm-Up
(From page 71):
(3) Marni Nixon provided the singing voice for Debra Kerr in *The King and I*, Natalie Wood in *Gypsy*, Rita Moreno in *West Side Story*, and Audrey Hepburn in *My Fair Lady*.

RICH IN RELATIONSHIPS (I)

INVESTING IN FRIENDSHIP

Strategy: The rich single life exhibits a love for others that produces meaningful friendships radiating the deep glow of fellowship.

BIBLE STUDY   1 John 3:1; 4:11

WARM-UP   A sitcom quiz: Draw lines to match the "Pals" with their respective main characters. The grand prize goes to anyone who can honestly say, "I have no idea who any of these people are."

Pals of the Main Character	Main Character
Floyd, Gomer, and Otis •	• Jerry Seinfeld, who played himself, sort of.
Lou, Rhoda, and Phyllis •	• Dick Van Dyke, who played Dick Petrie
Kramer, George, and Elaine •	• Andy Griffith, who played Andy Taylor
Buddy, Mel, and Sally •	• Mary Tyler Moore, who played Mary Richards

(See page 108 for answers)

PERSONAL STUDY   "It's a Wonderful Life" is my favorite movie of all time. For those of you who have never seen it (both of you), Jimmy Stewart plays George Bailey, an ordinary guy from Bedford Falls. Time after time, year after year, George gives up his dreams for the sake of his responsibilities. One Christmas Eve, life comes crashing in around him. When all he has built seems futile, George resolves to end his life by leaping from a bridge. At the last moment, Clarence Odbody, his guardian angel, steps in and shows him what life would be like in Bedford Falls if George had never been born. Through Clarence's intervention, George sees that because of his impact on others he truly is "the richest man in town." In the closing scene a grateful George picks up a book left for him by Clarence and reads the parting inscription, "Remember, no man is a failure who has friends."

That line is always a guaranteed tear-jerker in my family— I suppose because it rings so true. George Bailey discovers that sharing our lives with one another yields a value and richness far beyond even our greatest accomplishments. People everywhere want to make a difference in the lives of others and to experience the benefits of meaningful human relationships. We all want friendship.

Meditate on Ruth 1:1-18. How would Ruth's expression of commitment have affected Naomi following the loss of her husband and sons?

How deep does this desire run? In a recent poll of religious belief among people age 18 to 28, most said they felt it was more important to be accepted by others than to believe in God! The greatest needs that faith should meet, according to this group, include "not being judged," "avoiding ridicule," "finding an unshockable ear who will always love me no matter what," and having "someone who will always be there and never betray me."[2] As if anticipating the desperation for friendship expressed in this poll, Aristotle once wrote, "Without friends, no one would choose to live, though he had all other goods.[3]

1 At which of these church events would you find it easiest to meet new potential friends?

❑ Sports leagues and activities

❑ Service or evangelism events

❑ Large social gatherings such as picnics

❑ Small-group meetings

❑ Retreats

But what everyone wants, few can define. What is friendship? Who is my friend? Who is not? Do I need to change myself to be accepted by others, or should I demand acceptance on my own terms? Can only extroverts have friends? Does everyone need a "best friend"? Where can I find friends like the ones in the beer commercials? Questions like these can perplex and confuse us

90

in our attempts to experience that mystical thing called friendship.

Living a George Bailey Kind of Life

You as a Christian single are probably wrestling with some of these questions. Maybe you lack close friendships and aren't sure how to develop them. Maybe you don't know how to overcome problems in the friendships you do have. Maybe you've been hurt in a friendship gone bad and want to try to start over. My hope is that this study will provide helpful insights into the nature and purpose of friendships as the Bible defines them. The things we cover should apply to same-gender friendships, as well as friendships between men and women. In the next study we will look at male/female relationships as they move beyond being "just friends."

> ** God brings His own friends together in remarkable ways. He delights in a good friendship....Friendships cannot be over-emphasized in the single life. They should be many and varied, always growing in depth, always increasing in number.[4] **
>
> — **Margaret Clarkson**

The Essentials of Christian Friendship

Three essential characteristics distinguish a biblical approach to friendship from the secular approach that dominates our culture. Biblical friendship is initiated by God, governed by covenant, and designed for fellowship.

Initiated by God. One of the jarring truths of the Bible is that, apart from God's grace, no one can receive or give real love. I don't recommend sending that little nugget around the interoffice e-mail, but it is true nonetheless. As natural-born sinners wrapped up in self, we have nothing in us to generate a love that is not sin-infested and self-promoting. Scripture clearly shows that our ability to love comes from God. "This is love: not that we loved God, but that he loved us and sent his Son as an atoning sacrifice for our sins....We love because he first loved us" (1Jn 4:10,19). We all want to love and be loved, but our ability truly to do so begins with God's initiative and example of what love should look like.

Friendship is one specific expression of love from God; God often relates to his chosen ones as a friend (Ex 33:11, Jas 2:23). So, to enjoy true friendship, we must first

For Further Study:
Read John 3:16 and 1 John 3:16. What one idea connects these two verses with similar addresses?

> **"** Through him alone do we have access to one another, joy in one another, and fellowship with one another.[5] **"**
> — **Dietrich Bonhoeffer**

understand true love. Paul's familiar exposition on love in 1 Corinthians 13 provides ideal guidance on how to practice friendship God's way. For a fresh look at this passage, let's read a portion of it from Eugene Peterson's paraphrase of the New Testament:

No matter what I say, what I believe, and what I do, I'm bankrupt without love. Love never gives up. Love cares more for others than for self. Love doesn't want what it doesn't have. Love doesn't strut, doesn't have a swelled head, doesn't force itself on others, isn't always "me first," doesn't fly off the handle, doesn't keep the score of the sins of others, doesn't revel when others grovel, takes pleasure in the flowering of the truth, puts up with anything, trusts God always, always looks for the best, never looks back, but keeps going to the end. Love never dies.[6]

For Further Study:
Read 1 John 4:8-21. Why must those who love God also love their brother?

What are some practical implications of letting God's love define our friendships? Can we choose to befriend only people who seem to be compatible with us? Can we let prejudice tell us to avoid those who are not like us? Can we pursue friendships to improve our social standing? Can we test a friend's loyalty and then break off the friendship if he or she flunks the test? Can we just "not like" certain people? Clearly, the love of God in our hearts will war against any of these sinful motivations. Instead, in response to the love he has given us, Jesus calls us to a humble, sacrificial, and faith-filled adventure in love. As Jesus told his disciples, "Love each other as I have loved you. Greater love has no one than this, that he lay down his life for his friends" (Jn 15:12-13).

Governed by covenant. A covenant, like a contract or treaty, is a binding agreement between individuals. It contains promises and requirements and—if it is broken—consequences. There are more than 300 references to the concept of covenant in the Bible. The major biblical covenants include the Abrahamic, Mosaic, and Davidic Covenants. Most importantly, through his atoning death and resurrection, Jesus Christ established the New Covenant, which is the basis for our faith. In these great covenants God is the primary party. He both establishes the terms of the covenant and fulfills them.

For Further Study:
Read 1 Samuel 20. What promises were made by Jonathan and David in their covenant of friendship?

I find it helpful to think about friendship as involving a

kind of covenant "lite." As applied to friendship, covenant means those basic understandings underlying our relationships as Christians. (We'll discuss covenant as it applies to marriage in Study Eight.) Now, do we sign a pre-friendship agreement with everyone we run into in church? Of course not. Most often our "covenant" understanding is just that—an unspoken understanding of expectations and limitations between two people in relationship.

---

2 Which of the following assumptions (implied covenants) do you bring into your friendships?

❏ A friend will consistently return my phone calls

❏ A friend will tell me the things that trouble his/her heart

❏ A friend will remember the important things about me (like my birthday)

❏ A friend will know when to give me space

❏ A friend will_____ (fill in the blank)

We all make implied, covenant-like agreements all the time. If you drive me to a party, I can reasonably assume you'll give me a lift home, unless we agree (modify the covenant) otherwise. Have you ever given a gift and not received a thank you in return? Didn't you feel just a little put out? Why? Because you had an expectation that a gift received requires a thank you. It's not like you put on a little card, "This gift requires a written thank you on personal stationery within 72 hours." You just expect it.

Of course, the implied covenants in some friendships can become quite intense. There can be great expectations regarding how much time we'll spend together, how much free access I have to you, how you will treat me, and so on. Relationships like these have given rise to the concepts found in today's self-help jargon: co-dependency, toxic relationships, the need for boundaries, and the like. If you were to poke around the innards of a "co-dependent relationship," I think you would see a whole host of implied commitments and expectations that define the relationship—a friendship "covenant" gone berserk.

So the issue is not *whether* we form relational mini-

Meditate on James 2:23. Is there any reason you can't consider yourself a friend of God?

93

covenants, but whether we form them according to God's ways. Basically, God has a simple, all-purpose, three-word formula for Christian friendships: love one another. That's it. Jesus said it (Jn 15:17), Paul said it (Ro 13:8), Peter said it (1Pe 1:22), and John said it (1Jn 4:11). Of course, there is some fine print to this formula. I have given you a little of it in the selection from 1 Corinthians 13 above. (See 1 John 4:7-21 for the total package.) While loving one another God's way can seem overwhelming, let us remember that in both his empowering and his example, it is God who gives us the ability to love.

> **" Friendship between earthly friends consists much in affection; but yet, those strong exercises of affection, that actually carry them through fire and water for each other, are the highest evidences of true friendship.[7] "**
>
> **— Jonathan Edwards**

Covenant love binds us into relationships. If we develop our friendships and maintain them with covenant love, disagreements will never destroy them. We won't demand something from a friend that we can get only from God. If marriage enters the picture and we're the odd man out, we won't resent it; we will rejoice. If a friend stumbles in temptation, we will be faithful to continue to love him unconditionally, even while holding the standard of righteousness in plain sight. If a friend suffers loss, we will suffer with him: "A friend loves at all times, and a brother is born for adversity" (Pr 17:17). We will realize that in the family of God all relationships are eternal. Regardless of changes in status, location, or accessibility, we will faithfully honor a relationship in whatever way appropriate across the years.

Meditate on Ecclesiastes 4:9-12.
Are there any areas in your life where independence may be depriving you of important help through friendship?

I recently took my kids to the Mall area of Washington, D.C. As we walked toward the stark, sober granite of the Vietnam Veterans Memorial, I told them that relatives and friends of the deceased soldiers whose names cover "The Wall" often visit there. As we walked the path that runs alongside the memorial, we noticed a man sitting cross-legged next to it. He was weeping, deeply and unashamedly. We quietly passed by, and in a few minutes looked back. He was gone. Left in his place leaning against the wall was a small pad of paper. On the pad was scribbled the following message.

"Hi Dude, I bet you're surprised I'm here. I haven't forgotten you. Ever since that foxhole I've wondered why it was you that bought it and not me. I remember when they built this thing I swore I'd get here and find your name.

It's taken 20 years, but here I am. I miss you. I hope someday we'll hook up again, somewhere. Rock on, Bro."

I don't know if this vet was a Christian, but he understood something. He understood the value of shared humanity. He understood sacrifice. He understood the importance of commitment. To some degree, he understood covenant. May we as covenant friends love one another as God loves us.

Designed for fellowship. Christian friendship should produce fellowship. Notice I didn't say, "Christian friendship *is* fellowship." It's not. There are many aspects of our friendships that are enjoyable and beneficial, but which are not fellowship. I recently invited a friend over to play a Civil War computer game. For three hours we did battle. The only words spoken were about strategy, and lamentations when strategy went awry. It was an excellent time—intense, bonding, satisfying—a great memory for our mental scrapbooks. But it certainly wasn't fellowship.

> ❝ To reduce a Christian understanding of fellowship to drinking coffee after the service, engaging in recreational activities or the fulfillment of a particular work project, is superficial, if not erroneous. Such activities may stem from fellowship but are not fellowship in themselves.[8] ❞
>
> **— D.J. Tidball**

So what is fellowship? There is no way I can exhaustively discuss fellowship in this context, so let me recommend a great concise treatment of the subject by John Loftness in the book, *Why Small Groups?* In his study, "Fellowship Rediscovered," Loftness defines fellowship:

> [Fellowship is] participating together in the life and truth made possible by the Holy Spirit through our union with Christ. Fellowship is sharing something in common on the deepest possible level of human relationship—our experience of God himself.... Opportunities to fall in love, get married, procreate, pursue a career, go bungee jumping, play baseball, or go to school are all open to humanity in general. But only Christians can experience fellowship.[9]

Two truths stand out in this definition. First, *fellowship directly produces spiritual fruit in our lives*. Many activities can build friendships, but some of those activities may (and should) also help us grow as individual believers. We can't "do" fellowship, but we can experience it. Fellowship may result from something as pleasant as sharing a testimony or praying together, or from something as unpleasant as confessing our sin. Whatever the event, when God uses a friendship to increase my spiritual maturity, I have had fellowship.

---

3 In a typical one-on-one interaction, what percent of your behavior involves talking about and focusing on yourself, and what percent involves listening to and focusing on the other person? As a goal, what would you like the two percentages to be?

	Typical	**Goal**
Focus on me	_____	_____
Focus on another	_____	_____
Total	100%	100%

Because God is involved, fellowship can occur in unlikely ways. It doesn't even require relational closeness or a shared history—I can have deep fellowship with a Christian whom I have just met. Nevertheless, friendships remain vital to our relational diet because they give us the *best* and *most frequent* opportunities to experience fellowship. A lack of friendships will inevitably result in a lack of fellowship.

> **" Fellowship with God, then, is the source from which fellowship among Christians springs; and fellowship with God is the end to which Christian fellowship is a means.**[10] **"**
> — **J.I. Packer**

A second truth about fellowship is this: *Fellowship can only occur among Christians.* This is the major reason we ought never to let our closest relationships be with those who do not walk with Christ. Paul warns us of as much. "Do not be yoked together with unbelievers. For what do righteousness and wickedness have in common? Or what fellowship can light have with darkness?....What does a believer have in common with an unbeliever?" (2Co 6:14-16). You may love to hang out with the guys at the office, or with your sorority sisters from old Party U., but if these represent your primary friendship network, you'll get some good times, but you won't get fellowship.

Meditate on 1 John 1:1-4. How would John's personal experience of Jesus Christ have allowed him to experience deeper fellowship with others?

Please take a moment to think about your relationships. Do you get most of your relational enjoyment from hanging out with people who don't know Christ? Do you believe that career success requires you to focus primarily on business relationships? Perhaps you've tried to connect

Meditate on
1 Corinthians 15:33.
How should this verse
affect your choice of
friends?

with some Christians you know, but they seem to be less like you than your non-Christian friends, so you're tempted to go with what is more comfortable. The good pastor Charles Spurgeon encourages you, "In your choice of friends, choose those who are the friends of God."[11] Spurgeon's contemporary, J.C. Ryle, puts it a little more bluntly, "Never make an intimate friend of any one who is not a friend of God."[12]

My plea is that, in your relationships, you would value fellowship as your overriding goal. Only friendships in Christ can produce fellowship. Make these your primary investment.

Taking the 1 Timothy 4:12 Challenge

"The only way to have a friend is to be one." Here is a worn-out cliche—repeated by everyone from Ralph Waldo Emerson (who originated it) to Mr. Rogers—that actually has some biblical relevance. Paul says much the same thing in Philippians 2:4. "Each of you should look not only to your own interests, but also to the interests of others." Unlike credit-card applications, friendships don't just inundate you whether you ask for

> ❝ Friendship is not a reward for our discrimination and good taste in finding one another out. It is the instrument by which God reveals to each the beauties of all the others.[13] ❞
>
> — **C.S. Lewis**

them or not. Each believer carries a God-given responsibility to move beyond the cocoon of self in search of friendship. But how do we position ourselves to become the kind of friends God would have us be?

The Apostle Paul wrote two letters to a young man named Timothy. From his youth, Timothy had apparently been raised in the faith by Paul and was now a close associate and fellow pastor. By all indications, Timothy seems to have been a single man, probably in his thirties when Paul wrote to him. In the first of these pastoral letters, Paul encourages Timothy with the following, "Let no one look down on your youthfulness, but rather in speech, conduct, love, faith, and purity, show yourself an example of those who believe" (1Ti 4:12, NAS).

Some people apparently considered Timothy a pastoral lightweight, so Paul urges him to set a spiritual example. It may seem surprising that Paul doesn't focus Timothy on private pieties such as prayer and study. Instead, he

For Further Study:
Read Philippians 2:1-4.
List the ways Paul
encourages us to relate
to one another.

pushes him out into the nitty-gritty of the relational world. "Prove your stature by your love," he seems to be saying. You don't have to be called to be a pastor to see the relational value in Paul's instructions. This verse can be a kind of blueprint for how we can prepare ourselves to be the friends we ought to be.

Set an example in speech. Our speech has an amazing ability to reveal our hearts; it is the loud-speaker of our lives. It broadcasts who we are—for better or worse—far beyond our ability to control it. Our speech can alienate people or get us in a heap of trouble without our even knowing it. James warns us that the same tongue that blesses can curse as well (Jas 3:9-10). But our speech can also encourage, edify, and inform. Believers are encouraged to "let your conversation be always full of grace" (Col 4:6), and we're reminded that "the lips of the righteous nourish many" (Pr 10:21).

---

4 What is one statement your speech repeatedly makes about you that you regret? Here are a few sample entries to get you thinking:

❏ My motto is: Why should I ask a question when I can render an opinion?

❏ I am "The_Human_Internet@megabrain.com"

❏ If you can interrupt me when I stop to breathe, you can sometimes shut me up.

❏ Small talk is the best talk.

Write your entry in the space below:

What does your speech say about you? Are there any ways you speak that hinder your relationships?
• Do you express your pride by talking too much?
• Do you offend others by talking too loudly?
• Do you disrespect others by interrupting?
• Do you listen (as opposed to just taking a breath between paragraphs)?
• Do you ask questions or just state opinions?

• Do you complain?

• Do you argue?

• Do you gossip? Proverbs 16:28 says, "A perverse man stirs up dissension, and a gossip separates close friends." Gossip (like its cousin, slander) is the sharing of information about others which is not your business to share. The fruit of gossip and slander is always damage to reputations, relationships, and the cause of Christ. If you play the role of "water-cooler reporter" or "rumor central" among your friends, take a look at Romans 1:28-32 and 2 Corinthians 12:20. You'll see that the Bible puts gossip in with some pretty ugly company.

Meditate on Proverbs 17:9. How can you promote love when someone brings you gossip about someone else?

Gossip cannot be trivialized or overlooked. Scripture actually commands church discipline for unrepentant gossiping, and it is important to note that the Bible specifically warns single women ("unmarried widows" in the text) about the temptation to gossip (1Ti 5:13).

Why the emphasis here on the sin of gossip? Because most pastors will tell you that nothing destroys long-standing friendships and ruptures Christian community like gossip. Once gossip has been passed along, there is no way to undo its damage. Please don't do it, and don't tolerate it in your midst! If you are tempted to gossip, pray for that individual or situation instead. If you have gossiped, the only scriptural solution is to go to the people you have talked to—as well as to the person or persons you gossiped about—and confess your sin. If someone comes to you with gossip, put out the fire. Serve that person by gently confronting the sin, and help him or her to discern the best way to proceed. Call one another to a level of maturity, love, and trustworthiness that will make gossip rare in your midst.

> " Why, indeed, do we converse and gossip among ourselves when we so seldom part without a troubled conscience?[14]
>
> — **Thomas à Kempis**

Set an example in conduct. In 1 Timothy 4:12, "conduct" literally means "manner of life"—our accumulated habits, tendencies, quirks, and ruts. It's what we do when we aren't thinking about what we're doing. What does your manner of life say about what's important to you? Do people decline rides in your car rather than try to dig a way through the rubble? Does everybody leave your parties by 9:00 p.m. because they're fed up with you following them around shoving coasters under their glasses?

For Further Study: Read Philippians 1:27-28. How does our manner of life affect our witness to the world?

More importantly, what example do you set in your

99

**Meditate on
1 Corinthians 10:23-
24; 31-33.** How should
these passages influ-
ence the way you and
your friends relate to
movies, music, and
other cultural media?

ingestion of the prevailing culture? Do people come to you for reviews of the latest R-rated movies? Do your friends value you as a walking *People* magazine? Rather than being a cultural trend-setter, why not instigate among your friends a regular evaluation of your collective media intake? My friends and I often bring our tolerance for compromise in our media diet under the lamp of shared scrutiny. Paul gives some great guidelines in this area in 1 Corinthians 10:23-24; 31-33. Check them out.

Set an example in love. We have already discussed love extensively, so no need for further expansion here. One point of application, though. What is the "clique con-sciousness" of your church singles group? Are you an "inny" trying to maintain your "innyness"? Or are you an "outy" lobbing sarcasm bombs at the clique du jour? Does it really matter? While true cliques are factions—sinful institutions that must be dismantled—I have found that cliques often exist only in the eye of the beholder, and our preoccupation with them just distracts us from God's bet-ter pursuits. Set an example of love and move beyond the childishness of clique consciousness (see 1Co 13:11).

---

5 Romans 12:13 tells us to "practice hospitality." Which of the following is most like the kind of hospitality you practice?

"Sue held a formal state dinner last night..."

"Feel free to pick over whatever you find in the fridge..."

"Well, we can always watch a video..."

"Tonight's topic on "Point/Counterpoint" is..."

"Meet me in the chat room..."

**Meditate on Proverbs
27:6, 9.** Do you consid-
er the rebuke of a
friend a faithful wound
or an irritating jab? Do
you appreciate the
earnest counsel of oth-
ers regarding your char-
acter weaknesses? If
so, why?

Set an example in faith. In the 1 Timothy passage, "faith" means a personal devotion to God that works itself down into our attitudes and actions. This is not super-spirituality, but a street-level trust in God. One reliable indicator of our faith is our attitude toward receiving cor-rection from others. This acquired discipline will never make anyone's Top Ten list of favorite activities, but it is vital for our growth and friendships. A friendship that cannot sustain the weight of loving correction will never experience the heavier glory of fellowship. In fact, Puritan Charles Bridges counsels us that, "Rebuke, kindly, consid-

> **❝** Seems like you know when I need you
> Seems like He knows who to send
> You never come as a prophet
> Just an open-hearted friend
> Faithfully wounding my pride
> Bringing me back to His side
> Sharing the word that you hide in your heart
> You are a true friend, pointing me to Him
> Lifting my downcast eyes
> Turning my wandering gaze to the sky
> Proving your love again
> You are a true friend[16] **❞**
> — **Twila Paris**

erately, and prayerfully administered, cements friendship, rather than loosens it."[15]

Our goal should go beyond simply tolerating confrontation; by God's grace we can get to the point where we desire it, and even begin to see those who bring it as the best kind of friend. John Wesley demonstrated this in a reply to a letter of criticism received from someone he didn't even know. Wesley's gracious response indicates a depth of a faith that is attractive to all: "I am exceedingly obliged by the pains you have taken to point out to me what you think to be mistakes. It is a truly Christian attempt, an act of brotherly love....For what is friendship, if I am to account him my enemy who endeavors to open my eyes, or to mend my heart?"[17]

Set an example in purity. The word Paul used here literally means "moral purity and innocence." The same Greek word appears later in this letter, when Paul tells Timothy in no uncertain terms to relate to the young women "as sisters, with absolute purity" (1Ti 5:2). Later I will address some implications of this verse for courtship interactions, but its primary context has to do with the overall spectrum of relationships.

---

6 The 1 Timothy 4:12 Challenge calls us to grow in five relational areas. Rate the following areas by numbering them 1 through 5, where 1 is the area in which you are doing the best, and 5 being the area in which you need the most work.

Speech   Number: _____   Grade:_____

Conduct   Number: _____   Grade:_____

Love   Number: _____   Grade:_____

Faith   Number: _____   Grade:_____

Purity   Number: _____   Grade:_____

What *letter grade* would you give yourself in each area?

For Further Study:
Read Proverbs 22:11.
What personal charac-
teristics will give us
favor with others?

Brothers, it is in this matter of purity that you want to distinguish yourselves from the world in the clearest possible terms. The norm of the world is for men to be just a little dangerous, to preen and posture toward women so as to pique not only their curiosity, but a little apprehension, too. The kingdom man, by contrast, is defined by meekness—mature strength governed by a mature will. The meek will inherit the earth, and the pure in heart will see God (Mt 5:5,8). It is the pure quality in meekness that causes people to trust us implicitly, and to desire our friendship.

Handling Conflict: Life in Sanctification House

Many of the most mature, godly men and women in our church live in one of several single-gender households of up to five church members each. In some cases every member of such a household carries significant job and ministry responsibilities. You might think that bringing all this character and gifting under one roof would produce veritable oases of harmony and good cheer. Well, not exactly. It seems that in the house rules these folks somehow always forget to include "Thou shall not irritate thy fellow housemates." The result? Relational problems. We've come to call these our "Sanctification Houses"— you can enter, but you can't survive without changing.

Meditate on Colossians 3:12-17.
How can you and your household or friendship group apply Paul's instruction in this passage?

What makes a singles' household a Sanctification House is the same thing found in dorms, small groups, and singles ministries everywhere: conflict— the inevitable result of sinners walking out life together in friendship. How do you deal with conflict in your relationships? Do you withdraw and send out little "hurt" signals? Do you get angry and vengeful, and turn a conflict into a test of wills? Or maybe you keep all your relationships just superficial enough to dodge those pesky meaningful commitments that make you care about how you treat a friend?

> **❝** This is the message we have heard from him and declare to you: God is light; in him there is no darkness at all. If we claim to have fellowship with him yet walk in the darkness, we lie and do not live by the truth. But if we walk in the light, as he is in the light, we have fellowship with one another, and the blood of Jesus, his Son, purifies us from all sin. If we claim to be without sin, we deceive ourselves and the truth is not in us. If we confess our sins, he is faithful and just and will forgive us our sins and purify us from all unrighteousness.[18] **❞**
>
> — John the Apostle

No matter how we try to avoid the yuckiness of conflict (and I've tried almost every tactic), it *will* find its way into our friendships because our natural self-orientation to life is constantly inviting it to move in, rent-free. In Study Two we discussed how to deal with this permanent tendency to focus on ourselves. I'd like now to offer a few suggestions on how to handle such self-generated relational conflict biblically.

In this section I am deeply indebted to Ken Sande for his outstanding book, *The Peacemaker*. It is one of my perennial Top 5 recommendations to people I counsel. I'll just discuss some main points here (so make sure you read the book). *The Peacemaker* describes four biblical steps to resolving relational conflict.

Glorify God. During conflict, our habit should be to focus on the question, "How can I glorify God in this situation?" This instantly takes our focus off ourselves and places it on God, who provides answers to even the most difficult relational challenges. Purposing to glorify God sends us to the Scriptures for perspective, to our knees for help, and to the Cross for mercy. Focusing first on God allows his immensity to dwarf our immediate problems. If all parties to the conflict seek to glorify the Lord, the path to resolving disputes opens wide. Let's make glorifying God our greatest goal in our conflicts.

> **“** If you do not 'glorify God' when you are involved in a conflict, you will inevitably glorify someone or something else. By your actions you will show that you either have a big God or that you have a big self and big problems....If you do not focus on God you will inevitably focus on yourself and your will, or on other people and the threat of their will.[19] **”**
>
> — **Ken Sande**

Get the log out of your own eye. In Matthew 7:1-6, Jesus encourages us to first examine how *we* contribute to offense, and *then* focus on the other person's offense. Focusing first on our sin will lead us to humility, repentance, and mercy—things that God will bless. For a long time I interpreted this passage as saying, "If you want to gain the right to judge someone else's sin, judge your own sin first." I was looking for a license to judge! One day, in wrestling with this passage over a conflict of my own, I finally saw that the goal is not judgment but ministry.

Jesus is teaching that if you want to help someone with something harmful to him or her, you first need to deal with the thing that's harmful to you. During a conflict, the right to judge another person is never given to us. And the obligation to minister to one another is never removed.

For Further Study:
Read Matthew 18:15-22. Do you understand the biblical process for helping another person deal with his or her sin against you? Do you follow this process?

THE SEVEN A'S OF CONFESSION

How ironic that we can lose some of our best friends because we won't acknowledge our contribution to relational problems, or we do it so poorly that nothing really gets resolved! We must understand that it is very rare to have relational breakdown where all the fault lies with just one person. When we understand this, we will want to learn how to confess our sins to those whom we have sinned against. This is humility, a steady bridge of reconciliation on the road to fellowship. Ken Sande teaches The Seven A's of Confession, a great tool for how to acknowledge our sin. Here's an adaptation of this tool.

1. **Address** everyone involved. Often our sin is against one person. Other times, such as when we gossip, many people may be affected. We should "complete the circle of confession" by going to everyone we can who might have been affected by our wrongdoing.

2. **Avoid** "if," "but," and "maybe." The opportunity to confess can also be the opportunity to practice a little spin control. Don't let your confession of sin come out sounding like a plea bargain.

3. **Admit** specifically. Don't say, "I'm sorry I hurt your feelings." Say what you did to hurt the other person, such as, "I know my unkind words hurt you." It is usually best to confess using categories of sin from the Bible. Rather than saying "I was upset," say "I was angry." Trying to find a biblical term for what you have done can sharpen your sense of conviction.

4. **Apologize**. An apology is *not* giving a reason for your action, it's an acknowledgement of how your behavior affected someone else. To apologize is to own the damage you've done. This tells the offended party that you are not just embarrassed by your behavior, but grieved by its effect on others.

5. **Accept** the consequences. In the Old Testament, people who had sinned sometimes wore sackcloth and ashes to signify their awareness of the consequences of their sin. In a world that seeks to insure against all consequences of wrong-doing, we can make quite a statement of humility by accepting the legitimate fruit of our sin without complaint.

6. **Alter** your behavior. This is more commonly called repentance. Repentance isn't sorrow or emotional catharsis, it is a decision and attendant actions to change what is necessary to make sure the sin is not repeated. Repentance doesn't atone for our sin, but it does demonstrate our desire to "go and sin no more" (Jn 8:11).

7. **Ask** for forgiveness. Sometimes we can feel badly about what we've done and even admit it to the person we have wronged. But we can often forget to actually *ask* that person to forgive us. "I'm sorry" is an acknowledgment of our bad feelings, but it is not asking forgiveness. Also, be sure to *ask* forgiveness, never demand it. And realize it may take a person a while to be able to forgive us from the heart. To be forgiven is not a right you hold, it is an act of mercy by another toward you.

Go and show your brother his fault. At times this step has appealed to me, as if it's supposed to be the fun part. It's not, and even thinking that way reveals a sinful, holier-than-thou motivation. Nor is this step about venting my anger and bitterness. It nearly always takes two people—each contributing their sin—to create a conflict. So in any conflict there must be a way for the specific offenses to be expressed, acknowledged, and dealt with. By God's grace, we *can* confront the sins of others in a helpful, non-judgmental way. We can also go and ask someone whether he or she has an offense against us.

As I develop the humility to tell others clearly and graciously of their sins against me, the same humility allows me not only to hear their offense against me, but to seek to repent of it. As I grow in the sincerity and completeness of my confession to others, a wonderful thing begins to happen. I experience fellowship.

Go and be reconciled. During the Cold War, the United States had a policy toward communist countries known as détente—literally "relaxing of tension." If you're like me, you can live with conflict, it's the tension that gets on your nerves. But the Bible calls us to a far greater resolution than mere détente. It calls for reconciliation. Ken Sande says that to seek reconciliation is to "replace hostility and separation with peace and friendship"[20] Obviously, true reconciliation must involve the efforts of all parties to a conflict, so Paul encourages us, "As far as it depends on you, live at peace with everyone" (Ro 12:18).

There are many things we can do to pursue peacemaking. We can forgive the other person; resolve to speak well of him or her; remain open to any effort at reconciliation; or get someone else involved in the manner of Matthew 18:15-16. Even if all our efforts fail to produce mutual reconciliation, we can live in the peace that we have glorified God and loved the way Jesus loves us.

Meditate on Matthew 5:23-24. What should you do if you have a conflict with someone right before your Sunday church meeting?

The Hard-Won Prize of Friendship

Melanie is a member of our church, and a resident in a Sanctification House. She recently had an experience in friendship that seems like a great way to sum up what we have just covered. Here is Melanie's story.

"I had an acquaintance of about four years (we'll call her Mary) who needed a place to stay for four months until she graduated from college. She heard we needed a roommate and asked if she could move in. Due to past

conflicts with her during college, I was hesitant, but figured that she may have changed and that I, along with my other roommates, should give her the benefit of the doubt. (Already, I was thinking I was better than she was.)

> **May the words of my mouth and the meditation of my heart be pleasing in your sight, O LORD, my Rock and my Redeemer.**
> — **Psalm 19:14**

"Within two weeks of her arrival, she and I had four major conflicts. Each time, Mary froze up and would not discuss anything until she was ready to, while I wanted everything resolved instantly. This mismatch in resolution styles only compounded the problems.

"By the time the fourth conflict poked through the door, Mary was sorry she had moved in and I was kicking myself for letting her. After each falling-out I would sort of apologize for my part and sort of work a little harder to avoid conflicts. (The best way to do this was to not come out of my room in the morning until she left for work, and make sure I was in bed at night before she got home from class.)

"I got angry at the very thought or mention of her, and felt as if she definitely had a lot more apologizing to do before I could even be civil to her. I knew my words and actions were a poor testimony of my commitment to Christ. I am ashamed that, after walking closely with the Lord for nearly five years, this was the condition my heart was in, but I would be lying if I said otherwise.

"One weekend I unexpectedly realized that the only way this wall of resentment was going to come down was by me taking up my cross and dying to my pride and self-righteousness. Ouch!!! It hurt. It took three days of wrestling with God before I could do what I knew he was calling me to do. God clearly showed me through his word that I needed to humble myself for his glory, inside and out, and make amends with Mary by confessing the sin in my heart. I had to also demonstrate in a practical way that I was genuinely willing not only to forgive, but to love her as a sister in the Lord.

"I did not want to obey, but after a few days of praying (and crying), I knew it was time. It still was not easy, but I bought Mary a small gift and took it to her bedroom. I gave it to her, saying it was meant to symbolize a genuine effort at a new friendship, and I asked her to please forgive me for the selfishness I had displayed. She was very willing. We hugged for a long moment. When we *separated she informed me that she now had renewed hope for the friendship she had been desiring to build with me for a long while.*

"Since that day there has been nothing but harmony between us, and we enjoy spending time together. In two weeks it will be time for her to leave us and I can honestly say that, as a result of the work God has done in my heart, I will miss her dearly. I will carry this lesson with me forever and will give God the credit and honor due him. He prompted me to a step of spiritual growth and maturity, held my hand while I walked through the fire, and allowed me to experience the fullness of joy that comes only from submission and obedience to him. He has also given me a new friend!"

Taking a Cue from Clarence

There's a pivotal scene in "It's a Wonderful Life" where it begins to dawn on George Bailey that his life really is meaningless without the lives of others close to him. As the camera zooms in for a haunting close-up of George's tortured face, Angel Second Class Clarence Odbody reflects, "Each man's life touches so many other lives, and when he isn't around he leaves an awful hole, doesn't he?"

By the grace of God, Melanie and Mary are no longer absent from one another's lives. They have filled with hard-won friendship what was once a gaping hole between them. Whom does your life touch? Who touches you? Are there any holes in your relational network that can be replaced with meaningful fellowship? Invest in friendship. Be one to find one. ∎

GROUP DISCUSSION 1. How would you respond to the question, "What is the greatest need that faith should meet?"

2. How do you determine when a relationship has moved beyond acquaintance to friendship?

3. How did becoming a Christian affect your friendships?

4. Suppose your best single friend gets engaged. How should you relate to that person before and after he or she is married?

5. Suppose you were engaged to be married and your best single friend wasn't. How should you relate to your friend before and after you are married?

6. Describe the last time you experienced genuine fellowship with another person. What made it fellowship?

7. What is most needed in your present circle of relationships that would make your fellowship deeper?

8. What should you do as a Christian if you feel you are being excluded from a group of other Christians?

9. What are some ways to develop trustworthiness in a friendship?

10. What is your typical first *response* when you become aware someone is offended with you? What should your first *action* be?

11. Complete this sentence: "I can most easily receive correction from others if..."

12. After a conflict, how do you know when a relationship has been reconciled?

RECOMMENDED READING   *The Peacemaker* by Ken Sande (Grand Rapids, MI: Baker Book House, 1991)

When People Are Big and God Is Small by Edward T. Welch (Phillipsburg, NJ: Presbyterian and Reformed, 1997)

RICH IN RELATIONSHIPS (II)

COURTING RELATIONSHIPS

Strategy: The rich single life is prepared and willing to pursue a relationship toward marriage in submission to God's timing, wisdom, and Word.

BIBLE STUDY Philippians 4:19

WARM-UP In 1979 Rex Smith, a temporary teen idol (is there any other kind?), recorded a hit song entitled "You Take My Breath Away." The song is still heard regularly on oldies stations across the land. Approximately how many times in this two-and-a-half minute song is the title line sung?

1. Twenty-five to thirty times

2. Three times (once as the last line of each verse)

3. Eleven to twenty times

4. Five to ten times

5. It is never actually sung in the song

(See page 128 for answer)

PERSONAL STUDY We turn now to an issue that often preoccupies the attention, imagination, and fears of single adults—attraction to the opposite sex and the inevitable complications produced by that attraction. If you have skipped over the rest of the book to get to this part, hold on, Sport! Navigating the treacherous highway of romance can't be done recklessly. Everything discussed earlier in this book has a direct bearing on our ability to "feel the road." The vitality of our relationship to Christ, our vision for our maleness or femaleness, our growth in wisdom, our commitment to live for God's glory, and our ability to maintain good friendships are all foundational to building a healthy relationship with that person of the opposite sex with whom we would like to be "more than just a friend."

In this study we will look at the practical aspects of our

God-given interest in the opposite sex. First we will examine what a distinctly Christian world-view in this area looks like. Then we'll discuss some of the common questions men and women wrestle with as they view each other with specific intent.

Revisiting the Rituals of Romance

Here in Philadelphia we have an odd New Year's Day tradition. While most sane folks in the rest of the country are sleeping late or watching bowl games, thousands of people line our downtown streets in freezing weather to watch the 12-hour Mummer's Parade. What's a Mummer? I have no idea. I only know that the parade consists of a bunch of burly guys who look forward to once a year dressing in satin and sequins and spending the entire day strutting to music played by orchestras of marching banjo players. And the whole thing is televised!

Why do mummers mum? Don't ask me, but they've been doing it for years. It's a Philadelphia tradition, an annual ritual.

 Write down one holiday tradition that you perform without fail.

For Further Study:
Read Micah 6:6-8. What pleases God more than our ritual service to him?

Rituals are things we always do, often for reasons long forgotten. Holidays have a way of spawning rituals, seemingly at random. At Christmas, why do we give fruitcake, of all things? How did bunnies and baskets get tied into Easter? Rituals cause us to do odd things, like renting tuxedos, or paying twice as much for roses, turkeys, or pumpkins than we would at any other time of year. Now, with a little research you *can* find out, for example, where the idea originated for stacking brightly colored boxes under a dying, garishly decorated evergreen, but that basically has nothing to do with why we have Christmas trees today. We do it because...well...because at Christmas that's just what people do! In other words, because it's a ritual.

I believe the great ritual of singleness in America is dating. Why do singles date? The most accurate answer would probably be something profound like, "Because singles are supposed to date." Yet most people throughout history, and even throughout the world today, wouldn't understand dating any more than they would the Mummer's Parade. So why, in this culture and this era, do we promote dating like it's the only possible bridge across the gulf between the sexes?

Granted, men and women are very aware of each other, and they like to find ways to act on that awareness. There's no denying that. When I say dating is a ritual, I mean that we have developed an approach to opposite-sex relationships that no one is supposed to question. The ritual of dating essentially transforms male/female interactions into an elaborate game.

> " When I stopped viewing girls as potential girlfriends and started treating them as sisters in Christ, I discovered the richness of true friendship. When I stopped worrying about who I was going to marry and began to trust God's timing, I uncovered the incredible potential for serving God as a single. And when I stopped flirting with temptation in one-on-one dating relationships and started pursuing righteousness, I uncovered the peace and power that come from purity. I kissed dating goodbye because I found out that God has something better in store![1] "
>
> — Joshua Harris

The dating game is being played in a bar, Internet site, campus, or church singles group near you. It is a **marketing** game—I posture toward you, you flirt with me. It is a **competitive** game—guys compete among themselves for the attention of attractive women; women compare their attractiveness with that of other women; men and women compete with each other for control over the direction of the relationship. It is a **defensive** game—I seek your unwavering commitment even as I explore my options; I want your vulnerability without putting mine at risk.

Meditate on Colossians 3:15-17.
How does this perspective differ from the dating mentality?

Skill levels in the dating game are no small matter. How well we play usually dictates our success with the opposite sex. At least in the short term.

The biggest problem with the dating game is the results. Although most players are in some sense looking for a meaningful long-term relationship, few people ever realize that dating is not about the long term. As Douglas Wilson perceptively puts it, "The modern dating system does not train young people to form *a* relationship. It trains them to form a *series* of relationships."[2] As indicated by a 50 percent divorce rate, and many other marriages barely surviving, the dating game does not deliver.

Instead, the whole dating ritual is characterized by serial relationships (the "who I'm with right now" syndrome) and a general sense of hopelessness. Secular author and cultural critic Katie Roiphe sums up the frustration that many non-Christians are beginning to feel with the dating game.

Meditate on Philippians 2:1-4. How would Paul's strategy for relationships in this passage help you in a male/female relationship?

> It's hard when you can do whatever you want and no one cares. There's a feeling of exhaustion in having so many relationships—something a lot of people in their 20s feel when they've lived with three different people, dated 100 people, slept with 20 people. I think people are trying to create new meaning and importance, when now...they don't feel like they have any.[3]

Can the Game be Redeemed?

"But, of course," you may say, "I'm a Christian. I have Christian aerobics, Christian music, Christian jewelry, Christian video, Christian cruises (Christian books, too). Why can't I have Christian dating? If two people are Christians, shouldn't that take the problems out of dating?"

The lure of romance. Before you jump to that conclusion, think about the purpose of dating (which is also the reason it is so appealing): ***Dating exists to provide opportunities for turning casual interaction into romantic involvement.*** That's what dating does when it *works*. Now, romance is a great concept. It has an honorable place in marriage and makes for great poetry, but it's got serious pitfalls for single Christians.

By its nature, romance is emotional, disorienting, obsessive—and that's the good part. Romance is like race-car fuel. It burns very fast and hot. It's also very expensive. Great for stock cars, lousy for your daily commute. Romance is a volatile thing that by its very nature is unable to keep a relationship running smoothly and steadily along the road to lasting commitment. Did you ever wonder why romance stories always end either with a wedding or the tragic death of one of the lovers? Because lasting relationships take work, not just feelings. No one

For Further Study:
Read 1 Thessalonians
4:1-8. What are some
motivations provided in
this passage to help
you avoid sexual
temptation?

would pay to see the dashing young hero and heroine in a conflict over balancing the checkbook, because that's not romance. But it is reality.

Sexual temptation. A second snare of dating for the single Christian is sexual temptation. Dating that is "successful" produces romance, and romance is the fast track to sexual involvement. For Christians desiring purity in their lives and relationships, pursuing romance is like skydiving without a parachute; it just doesn't matter how nice the free fall is—God's law of spiritual gravity will not be broken, and soon, my friend, you're going to hit the ground at a very high rate of speed. Nothing does such violent damage to our walk with God, or our relationships with the opposite sex, as sexual temptation and sin.

> **❝** We're in the sexual promised land now...and yet we're starved for love....The acceptance, even encouragement of pre-marital sex makes it very difficult to sustain the fantasy that we are loved alone.[4] **❞**
>
> — Jennifer Grossman

Weighed in the balance. A third snare of dating is its emphasis on performance. Much of the dating ritual involves evaluation—am I attracted to you, are you attracted to me? This places a high priority on first impressions. But what if I put my best foot forward, present myself for approval, offer to pursue a relationship, and am rejected? In effect, I've been told "at your best you are unappealing." That's the kind of rejection that must be risked in order to play the dating game. For the Christian single who wants to glorify God, a risk like that represents (at best) unwise stewardship of one's time, attention, and vision; it's poor discipleship.

**Meditate on
1 Timothy 2:9-10.** How
does this passage
speak to your fashion
consciousness?

2 Rank the following ways to meet a potential Christian mate in the order of how helpful they would probably be: 1 being most helpful, 6 being least helpful.

_____ A Christian dating service

_____ A multi-church social function

_____ An on-line chat room

_____ An introduction through Christian friends

_____ Serving in ministry with other Christians

_____ Wearing a T-shirt that says: "Single, Serving God, Seeking a Mate"

The myth of compatibility. Occasionally a dating relationship survives the performance stage, only to run smack into another pitfall: the myth of compatibility. Because dating supposedly allows us to find this relational nirvana, our dating turns into a quest for anything we might have in common. We'll even try to invent commonalities where they don't exist. "Oh, you like ancient Greek allegorical drama? I've always been curious about that."

Meditate on Matthew 1:18-25. How might Joseph have reacted differently to Mary's predicament if he had been motivated by compatibility?

Is compatibility really some mysterious, indefinable magnetism that binds people together? I don't think so. What the world calls compatibility is simply a misleading label for those times when two people each find enough wants met in a relationship to make it worth sustaining. Such "compatibility" is very shaky. For it to remain, neither of us can change much. If my wants change in a way that you cannot adapt to, we are no longer compatible. The elusive sprite of compatibility has slipped through our fingers, and all we have left are "irreconcilable differences." Nirvana has gone AWOL.

The payoff of dating is the volatility of romance, the temptation of sexual sin, the superficiality of performance, and the myth of compatibility. No wonder more and more singles—Christian and non-Christian alike—are opting out of the dating scene altogether. It simply doesn't deliver the goods.

Liberated from the Game

Does this mean that anyone who rejects the ritual of the dating game must sit passively in desperate hope that God will somehow dump a sure-thing relationship into his or her path? For Christian singles who desire to explore whether God would bring them into a relationship that could lead to marriage, what's the alternative to dating?

In the previous study we looked at friendship, the starting point of any good male/female relationship. In the next study we will consider the implications of marriage, the biblical fulfillment of the desire of men and women for each other. What is needed is a link between these two states—a way for two friends of the opposite sex to begin to explore the possibility of a deeper relationship, one that might lead to marriage.

This relationship won't look like other friendships, but it can't look like a marriage, either. It needs to be flexible enough to allow for great diversity in personalities and situations, yet it must be strongly anchored to biblical truth. It must promote the things God values—honesty, respect, and love. It must resist the things the world values—selfishness, lust, and control. And it must allow for our mistakes and inconsistencies, for none of us can manage the ways of our hearts, let alone the heart of another, without some blunders.

If you are interested in labels, my current favorite for this type of relationship, this link between friendship and marriage, is a "courting relationship." I like the word courting because it speaks of a formal pursuit and response. I like the word relationship because it involves two people getting to know one another with increasing familiarity. *The distinguishing characteristic of a courting relationship is that it draws people close with the potential for marriage clearly in view.*

---

3 Can you come up with another possible label for what this book calls a "courting relationship"? Write it in the space below.

For the remainder of this study I will be providing some basic counsel for courting relationships. But first a word about rules.

People who come to our church often ask me, "What are your dating rules here?" They are typically somewhat surprised when I tell them we don't have any. Rules require referees, and I have no interest in refereeing relationships. As a pastor, I want to help each person as best I can to follow God throughout his or her life. For many people that means following God into (and sometimes out of) relationships. To me, the character and devotion needed to walk out a courting relationship is really no different than what is needed to walk out a vocation or ministry responsibility. My faith is not in some system of rules, but in God's ability to lead two obedient disciples along his chosen path.

Below are some of the Frequently Asked Questions regarding male/female relationships. I have tried to

Meditate on Proverbs 30:18-19. What do these four amazing things have in common?

For Further Study: Read Psalm 16:5-11. What blessings of walking with God are described in this passage?

answer them with the kind of responses I would give in pastoral ministry. These are not sure-fire, take-it-to-the-bank answers, but principles of wisdom that have proved beneficial to folks over the years. Proverbs talks about the wisdom found in an array of counsel. This can be part of your array. My hope is that these brief answers will help you form a biblical perspective that can serve you in any courting relationship that comes your way.

How can I prepare myself for a courting relationship? Some of the single sisters in my church used to have a little inside joke. When they saw a friend dieting or going to the gym, they would say she was "getting her house in order." They were gently teasing that she was trying to prepare herself for a potential relationship. Getting your house in order goes beyond getting presentable. It means putting yourself in the best position possible to respond to God's leading toward marriage.

For Further Study:
Read 2 Timothy 2:20-22. What are some ways Paul encourages us to prepare for any good work?

For single guys, getting your house in order often can mean identifying a sense of vocational direction. This doesn't mean a guy must be pulling down a six-figure salary to be eligible for marriage. But if he is aimless in his employment or has poor work habits, how can he ask a woman to entrust herself to his provision? Women also need a sense of vocational call, even if they eventually plan to be homemakers, because a directionless life tends to be a slothful life. Things like personal organization, control of debt and spending, consistent spiritual disciplines, and a servant's heart can also prepare a Christian for the potential of marriage. A few basic social graces can't hurt either.

> **❝** Biblical preparation for marriage is nothing more than learning to follow Jesus Christ and to love one's neighbor. In other words, preparation for Christian marriage is basically the same as preparation for Christian living. [5] **❞**
>
> — **Douglas Wilson**

How do I evaluate whether someone I am interested in would make a good marriage partner? Basically, if someone is following Jesus Christ and demonstrating mature love toward others, he or she probably has the makings of a good marriage partner. More specifically, there are two basic qualities I recommend for evaluation, based on my observation of successful and unsuccessful relationships.

A woman should evaluate a man's *respect for authority*. In our society, the godly man is most distinct from the worldly man in the way he has put away prideful independence and pursued humble submissiveness. A man who is independent in his faith and does not seek the counsel and oversight of pastors and other mature men, will be a failure as a leader (and therefore as a husband) as defined by Scripture. See the story of Abigail and Nabal for a sad example of an arrogant man not worthy of his virtuous wife (1Sa 25).

A man should evaluate a woman's *submission to Scripture* as her ultimate authority in life. Women live among competing authorities—domineering males, feminist rhetoric, deep emotions, worldly temptations. A godly woman will be a woman of the Word. She will know it, love it, and allow it to be the ruling authority in her life. As much as most women desire marriage and family, married women must embrace changes of identity and personal autonomy of a kind that men can't comprehend. If a woman trusts the teaching of God's Word regarding her identity and worth, she will enter the new world of marriage roles and responsibilities with abiding faith.

Meditate on: 1 Peter 5:5-7. In what ways can you develop the humility of a submissive attitude to authority?

---

4 Put a check by each item you would NOT consider to be a minimum requirement in evaluating someone for a potential courting relationship.

❑ Must have reliable transportation

❑ Must know the purpose of the outside fork in a formal place setting

❑ Must be able to parse first-century Greek

❑ Must have recent physical and lie detector test results available for review

❑ Must have style, a daffy personality, and sitcom looks

❑ Must either own a beach house or have country club privileges

❑ Must love/not love football (circle one)

❑ Must have teeth (good dentures OK)

❑ Must be a patient listener

Should single adults actively pursue a mate, or passively wait for someone to just sort of appear? A single brother once asked me a great question: "I've always thought my future wife would be in this church, but there is no one here I'm interested in. Is it wrong to look elsewhere? Is it 'seek and ye shall find' or 'wait on the Lord'?"

THEY SAY...

Most of the basic challenges in communicating with the opposite sex come from a two-way lack of understanding of our differences. As a public service, the following clues are offered to the confused, courtesy of that mysterious group of experts known only as "They." No one knows who "They" really are or how "They" come about their profound wisdom, but that doesn't stop us from quoting "Them" at every chance. So, the next time you hear anyone start a sentence with "They say..." you'll have your own group of They-isms to toss knowingly into the conversation.

Lost in Space

Next time you're at a gathering of singles, see if you can spot these tendencies. "They" say that men generally find security in open space, while women are more comfortable in close contact with others. So when women enter a room, they tend to sense the environment and find a comfortable place in it. Men go into a room, stake out a position, and then try to figure out what is going on around them.

What it means to be alone is also radically different for men and women. "They" describe aloneness for a woman as having no one *who understands you* nearby. For a man, aloneness is not having *anyone* standing nearby. Does this explain how men can bond on a golf course without saying a word, while women consider going to the bathroom a communal opportunity?

The Trouble with Talk

Why don't men and women understand each other? "They" say it's because we have different goals in conversation. To men, words are tools, things that are needed to get points across. The goal is to find the right tool for the right problem. Women use words to paint pictures, to reveal themselves, and to encourage others to reveal themselves. A man listens to gather ideas. A woman listens to share in an experience. Men are more comfortable talking in groups; women thrive in one-on-one situations. "They" also say women tend to be more successful than men at reading people's emotions, but men are stronger at spotting deceptions.

Biological Trivia That May-or-May-Not-Say-a-Lot Department

Women have more sensory nerve endings in their skin. Men compensate by having more sweat glands.

The Final Word

"The ugly truth about beauty: Women seek perfection. Men seek socks that match." (Dave Barry)

Meditate on Psalm 119:105. What has more impact in your life — what you feel or what the Bible says?

Meditate on Psalm 27:13-14. When it comes to trusting God for a spouse, how can you be strong, take heart, and wait?

Christian dating services, Internet chat rooms, and social clubs have proliferated largely due to the awareness that one's future mate may not be in the present geographic location or relational network. In many churches the pool of eligible singles is shallow. If it's fine to look for a job outside our circle of church contacts, why not do the same with relationships? Isn't the search for a potential mate far more important? (After all, you can always change jobs.)

There is nothing in the Bible that comes anywhere close to suggesting that you shouldn't seek a mate outside your local church. The issue you must focus on, however, is the heart issue of patience, not the practical issue of geography. Are you patient to wait for God's provision, or is unbelief driving you to undertake a desperate hunt?

God brought Rebekah to Isaac from another land. He gave Ruth a husband when she was a virtual outcast in a foreign land. God can bring a mate to you in the fellowship hall or in the mall. Just this past year I performed the wedding ceremony of a couple who had been childhood friends. They moved apart, and eventually both became Christians. They ran into each other one year while Christmas shopping back in their home town, renewed a friendship, and are now husband and wife.

Let me note, however, the significant courtship benefits that can flow from two singles having a common church experience. Similar values and vision, a supportive church-family environment, and consistent pastoral care can be very valuable to a couple in a courtship relationship. Also, some methods available for seeking a mate in the Christian community at large aren't always wise options, or ought to be approached with discernment, prayerfulness, and accountability. It's best to get mature Christian counsel regarding the range of options available to you.

The most important thing to remember in all this, however, is that whatever we leave in God's hands to accomplish will always work for our good. Until then the outer work of getting your house in order and the inner work of persevering prayer should keep you busy and focused.

How do two Christian friends start to develop a courting relationship? If two people have an ongoing friendship among a larger group of friends, it is usually not too hard to bump things up to a more intentional level. If you don't travel in the same social circles, a man should probably demonstrate his willingness to assume responsibility by making his intentions known. Perhaps a cup of coffee at a restaurant after a meeting is a good, safe way to begin.

It's always a good idea, however, to take advantage of group contexts whenever possible. Group interaction minimizes romantic pressures and allows friendships to develop naturally over time. Good communication is also important—not delving deeply into your personal lives, or discussing where you always wanted to go on a honeymoon, but regular interaction about where the relationship is and how each person is handling it. When feelings try to lead us in any number of directions, this kind of communication can keep reality and focus in the relationship.

A healthy relationship breathes freely. It can move forward easily, slow down, or even back up without great gnashing of teeth by either person. If both parties purpose to be known for modesty, integrity, and dignity in the relationship, it will mature with time, avoiding emotional catastrophes or the ruin of a perfectly good brother/sister friendship.

How do I invest in a relationship without getting hurt? When venturing into a courting relationship, we must face two realities. First, no formula can guarantee success. Male/female relationships defy scripting. They always have. Second, the process will inevitably involve some degree of emotional trial or pain. If you want a pain-free relationship, get a goldfish. Investing in a higher life-form, like a fellow sinner of the opposite sex, will always involve the potential for conflict and hurt. (As Christians, the difference is how we handle it: see Study Six.)

> **44** I have found that a man will usually be as much of a gentleman as a lady requires, and probably no more.[6] **77**
>
> — **Elisabeth Elliot**

Meditate on Proverbs 22:3. What are some danger signs in a relationship indicating that, if we keep going, we are likely to suffer?

---

5 Before reading the next paragraph, write three ways you can guard your heart in a courting relationship.

1.

2.

3.

Guard your heart. "Above all else, guard your heart, for it is the wellspring of life" (Pr 4:23). Guarding your heart means recognizing that your heart first belongs to God. You guard it because it is his property, not your own! Affection for another should never overtake our affection for God. God has given us a heart to be a wellspring, a place where his Spirit should have free reign. Guard your heart by resisting and rejecting infatuation and fantasy. Don't reorder your life and relational network around a new relationship. Let convictions rule your behavior.

Relate with purity. While the heart is the wellspring of life, it can also be deceitful and strongly inclined to sin (Jer 17:9). So be sure to apply the advice Paul offered his younger friend Timothy, and relate to the opposite sex with "absolute purity" (1Ti 5:2). This means that, as we relate to each other across gender lines, we must never be satisfied with the standards of our innocence. Purity starts in the heart and works its way out into our actions, attitudes, and words. We must continually ask God to convict us of impure motives and actions, for purity is absolutely vital to a healthy courting relationship.

Meditate on Proverbs 25:28. How does self-control come into play in protecting both yourself and the other person in a relationship?

Avoid exclusivity. When I see a man and woman pair off to the exclusion of other relationships—either spending a great deal of time together alone, or turning away from other friends toward each other—I know we are about to witness either an explosion or a meltdown. *No courting relationship should so warp our existing lifestyle that, if it were to end, we wouldn't have anything or anybody to go back to.*

> **❝** The only place outside Heaven where you can be perfectly safe from all the dangers and perturbations of love is Hell.[7] **❞**
>
> **— C. S. Lewis**

If we guard our hearts, relate with purity, and avoid exclusivity, we won't eliminate the potential for pain, but we can prepare ourselves to experience growth toward God through it.

How do the roles of leadership and submission work in a courtship relationship? A single woman once said to me, "I really believe my relationship can work, but he won't lead. What can I do?" My advice was, "If he won't lead, don't try to follow." This woman eventually came to realize that she was seeking leadership from a brother who was not ready for the responsibility. No amount of propping up or encouraging was going to make things work in such a situation.

Please understand this: The biblical roles of leadership

and submission in a relationship are covenantal. That is, they require a covenant of marriage in order to work. There is no ultimate biblical responsibility for a man to lead a woman, or a woman to submit to a man, in any personal relationship outside the covenant of marriage. This doesn't mean that a man shouldn't express a tendency to accept responsibility and leadership initiative, or that a woman shouldn't incline to be responsive to the man's direction and tone in a relationship. But single men and women stand in single status before the Lord and will therefore answer for their *personal godliness*, not their leadership or submission in a courting relationship.

Let me offer some practical advice. Brothers, I think good leadership initiative means you will be the one to assume responsibility for where a relationship is at any given time. Don't require a woman to show her cards for you to take the next step. Be willing to play your cards first and let her respond. Ask the Lord for grace to govern the relationship with wisdom and vision.

Sisters, don't *ever* abdicate your responsibility to hear from God for yourself regarding a relationship. No matter what a man says or does, you have to answer to God for your own decisions, and God will give you the grace to make them. Christian women who have been hurt in a relationship often realize that they brought some of the pain on themselves by assuming that God's will would be dictated through a man's actions. They realize too late that they foolishly avoided their personal responsibility in the relationship. If a single man is not earning the respect of a single woman by his character and conduct, it is simply unwise to assume that his behavior is an indication of God's will. Save yourself the heartache, and accept your responsibility to be obedient to God in any relationship you enter into.

How much physical affection is appropriate in a courtship relationship? A pastor I know recommends a simple and highly effective formula. We should ask for as much physical affection from someone we are courting as we would allow someone to have with our future spouse. There is great truth to this formula. Until we have uttered the great "I do" and been duly wed before God and man, we have no right to indulge any sexual desires or to draw any sexual desires out of another person.

So how much is too much? Just remember the absolute-purity standard that Paul gave to Timothy. Any physical expression that compromises either person's purity violates this biblical standard. Just because I'm comfort-

For Further Study:
Read 1 John 2:12-14. What kind of example is John affirming in the young men?

For Further Study:
Read 1 Corinthians 6:18-20. When we give in to sexual temptation, whom do we sin against?

able with some "innocent" behavior doesn't give me a right to tempt someone else. Is this strict? Yes. Is it wise? Extremely.

Activities that fail to honor the purity standards of Scripture will compromise the godliness of a relationship. Physical affection tends to squelch communication—it's easier to touch than talk. It also opens the door to deception, selfishness, and manipulation by redirecting the focus from what's best for the other to what feels good to me.

> ❝ When have I gone too far in a physical relationship before marriage? When my heart is pounding like a jackhammer and my hormones are flowing like water through a firehose, it's a pretty strong clue that I have gone too far already! At such times, my body neither knows nor cares about my Christian convictions. Instead of trying to figure out how to derail a fifty-ton locomotive traveling at high speed, wisdom suggests we would do better to stay off the train and avoid the crisis in the first place.[8] ❞
>
> — **Randy Alcorn**

Most of all, opening the door to a physical relationship tampers with God's blessing. Paul advises us, "Flee from sexual immorality...Do you not know that your body is a temple of the Holy Spirit, who is in you, whom you have received from God? You are not your own; you were bought at a price. Therefore honor God with your body" (1Co 6:18-20). Set your standard of purity high, and your tolerance for physical compromise low. Honor God with your relationship.

---

6 Many Christians advocate dating rules for handling courtship situations. Some of these rules are biblically wise and some are not. Put a check by each of the following rules that are scripturally supportable.

❑ Relate to each other with purity

❑ Never get involved in ministry with someone you find attractive

❑ Anything you do is OK as long as you pray before or after it

❑ Don't lead each other on

❑ Never interact outside of a group context with someone you are interested in

❑ As you pursue a relationship, have someone hold you accountable

---

How do I know if our relationship should lead to marriage? This is the million-dollar question. Sorry—no simple answers here. Marriage is one of the few for-life decisions a person will ever make. No one ever made a mistake trusting in Christ, but we can really mess up a marriage decision.

Does that feel heavy? It should. But my confidence is that in matters of such gravity, God will not leave Christians hanging. God definitely knows what he's doing (even if you don't just yet). He has been bringing men and women together ever since the garden of Eden. He prepares each of his children for a high calling, and for many that calling includes marriage. If you are called to marriage, trust God for the timing and submit to his training, and you will stand with the spouse of his choosing in the time of his blessing.

> 〝 Let the whole of your life be seen to be controlled by your concern for the glory of God. The kind of partner that will be suitable for you will be the kind of partner that recognizes and appreciates someone who is seeking first the Kingdom of God and his righteousness. Aim to be a man or woman of prayer, one who delights to walk closely with God, one who delights to walk in the ways of God. Let your whole life reflect the reality that you are a son or daughter of the King.[9] 〞
>
> **— Andrew Swanson**

From the moment I met my future wife, I felt we were supposed to be married. There were only two small problems: we lived in different parts of the country, and I was an immature Christian with no job. My bright idea was to take a foolish step of presumption (at the time I preferred to call it "a bold step of faith") and just get married. By God's grace, I had a wise pastor who helped me keep my immaturity in check. It took three years of Jill and I being apart before God brought us together to be married. I needed every bit of that time to get ready—any sooner, and I would have been unprepared. God took care of Jill and me. He'll take care of you, too.

For Further Study:
Read Matthew 6:25-34. What should be our focus as we wait for God's will concerning a life partner?

What happens if I am in a courtship and I realize it is not meant to result in marriage? Courtship is not a science, it's a relationship. Two people can do everything right, carry on an exemplary courtship, get along great, resolve any disagreements and conflicts that might pop up along the way—but none of this *necessarily* means that God wants them to be married. Sometimes, one or both of the people involved realizes the relationship is not meant to progress any farther. What to do then?

If two people have purposed from the beginning to walk humbly, submit themselves to God's timing and

For Further Study:
Read Philippians 4:10-13. What is Paul's secret in handling the difficult situations of life?

plan, and love as brothers and sisters until God defines them as more than that, the end of a courtship need not be traumatic. This is because true courtship is founded on friendship. To move from courtship back to friendship is therefore not a "break-up," just a re-definition. (The whole concept of breaking up derives from the world's hopelessly flawed dating rituals.) In a healthy courtship, the fundamental brother/sister friendship doesn't change. Therefore, when such a courtship does not end in marriage, there may be awkwardness and sadness, but there is still a good place for the relationship to go, and godly, responsible new roles to be played by each person.

Ultimately, it takes faith to open the door to a potential courting relationship. Not all such relationships will end in marriage. Those that do we will celebrate. Those that do not we can celebrate as well, because the same faith in God's guidance and will is required to move a courting relationship toward marriage or return it to godly friendship. In either case, the result is a testimony to the marvelous grace of God at work in his people.

> ❝ Because all believers are united to Christ and are members of His body, breaking off a [courting] relationship only changes the direction of that relationship, not its status.[10] ❞
>
> — Jeffery S. Forrey

Several years ago I was involved in the singles group of a small church. In that group were a man and woman who had at one time been engaged to one another. Since we were a small group, these two were constantly having to interact. But because they had walked out the relationship with integrity and ended it with respect, they had begun to see the shoots of a new friendship emerging from what had been the remains of a long courtship.

When the woman subsequently married another man in the group, my friend had to welcome that relationship into his life as well. It wasn't easy, but he knew he had walked in a way that pleased the Lord, so he had no regrets and was able to extend grace and love toward this new couple. In a world of bitterness and broken hearts, this kind of love makes a difference. It did for me, for it profoundly shaped my view of the potential of Christian courtship.

But Can It Work for Me?

This past year I have been honored to perform a number of weddings of people in our singles group. Included among the couples were two never-married single parents, a widowed single mother, a woman who had been abandoned in her first marriage, and several folks who had written off any hope of marriage. Nancy and Doug were one of those couples. Both in their late thirties, they had been stalwarts in our singles ministry for years. Both had been in courting relationships in the past, but those relationships had not worked out. Let me close with their story of God's leading, in Nancy's words.

"Doug and I met nearly ten years ago at a Bible study. We both remember going out for coffee one night after the study and talking for hours. I remember that Doug 'scared the life out of me.' It was as though he could see right through me, and I did not like that idea. So, for the next nine years as our friendship grew, I was always making sure we never got too close. The times we talked were wonderful, but afterward I would intentionally hide from him by keeping myself busy with other friends. If you were to ask my roommates, they'd tell you my favorite saying was, 'I just don't want him to like me!'

"From Doug's perspective, there wasn't any reason for me to hide. He was just being himself. His wonderful, friendly, inquisitive self, I might add...and of course, he was always a gentleman. About two years ago, I had a dream about Doug and was awakened with this overwhelming feeling of being totally loved, accepted, and known. It was beautiful, not scary. As I began to pray, I realized I had closed my heart years earlier to the idea of Doug and I ever being more than friends. God gave me the desire and the ability to stop hiding and to really become a good friend to Doug. The more I knew him, the more I loved him.

"However, it wasn't all easy. Doug did not have the same feelings for me. He regularly told me how much he respected and admired me, but there were no 'romantic feelings.' By the grace of God, we were able to grow in our friendship without any expectation of being more than friends. (I must admit I had lots of prayer partners, though.) And unbeknownst to me, the Lord was working in Doug's heart, too. I'll never forget the night last September when he told me, 'The seat next to you on the roller coaster isn't empty any longer' and asked me to walk out a courting relationship. These past eleven months have definitely been a roller coaster for both of us, but we know in our hearts there is no one else we'd rather ride next to than each other. 'The Lord is good to those who wait for Him.'"

A little postscript to the story. You might think that after all those years Doug and Nancy would be tempted to sprint into marriage without as much as a backward glance at their single friends. Not so. They remembered how hard it had been to be single and be guests and even attendants at the weddings of friends over the years, wondering if they would ever get the chance to wear the bride and groom clothes. In their joy, they did not forget the wait. At the end of their wedding service, each single woman received a rose, along with a note from Nancy that read:

Dear Single Sister,

Please receive this flower as an expression of God's love for you and his faithfulness to you. So many times I've gone to weddings and after the bouquet toss felt very lonely and sad. I promised myself that if I ever got married I would give each single woman a flower to honor her. I hope that our wedding has been a testimony to you of God's goodness and his perfect timing. Be encouraged...his way is perfect!

Brothers and sisters, even the big question of who you are to marry and how that will come about is not a perplexity to God. Prepare for the future, and love with purity and wisdom. Be encouraged. His way is perfect. ■

GROUP DISCUSSION
1. Is flirting OK for Christians? Why or why not?

2. At what point in a courting relationship is romance appropriate?

3. In what ways do men and women differ in their perspective on courting relationships?

4. What are some of the pitfalls of allowing first impressions to determine your perception of another person?

5. How can the unwise pursuit of a relationship have a negative effect on your Christian life?

6. How can you get to know someone well enough to determine whether you should pursue a deeper relationship with him or her, *without* spending lots of time alone together?

7. How important is it to keep the potential for marriage in mind when developing a deeper relationship with someone?

8. Whose responsibility is it to keep a relationship morally pure?

9. How can you know when you are ready to pursue a courting relationship?

10. What are some convictions you hold regarding how you will conduct yourself in courtship?

RECOMMENDED READING

Passion and Purity by Elisabeth Elliot (Old Tappan, NJ: Fleming H. Revell, 1984)

I Kissed Dating Goodbye by Joshua Harris (Sisters, OR: Multnomah Books, 1997)

RICH TOWARD MARRIAGE

Strategy: The rich single life embraces a biblical vision for marriage with sober but faith-filled anticipation.

BIBLE STUDY   Proverbs 31:10; 30-31

WARM-UP   The 50th Wedding Anniversary, the "Golden Anniversary," is so named because the traditional gift on that occasion is gold. Which of the following is NOT traditionally given for wedding anniversaries during the first ten years of marriage?

1. Nylon
2. Rubber
3. Tin
4. Plastic

(See page 144 for answer)

PERSONAL STUDY   A friend of mine, a pastor, was a guest at the wedding of one of his nieces, whom he did not know very well. Because weddings, for him, often involve carrying some degree of responsibility, he was more than happy to be just a spectator on this occasion. He was enjoying himself so much he didn't even realize the start of the ceremony was now long overdue. Suddenly there came a tap on his shoulder. Turning around, he saw his tuxedoed brother, the father of the bride. This could only mean trouble.

I Do What???

In a brief huddle at the back of the church, my friend learned the officiating clergy had failed to show, so he had been nominated as Emergency Clergy in Relief. OK, he could handle this. The first order of business, of course, was to have the bride and groom fill him in on what kind of service this was supposed to be. After a few moments of conversation with the somewhat jittery couple, however, he came to an unnerving conclusion—*THEY had no idea what kind of service this was supposed to be, either!*

This bride and groom had gotten to the very threshold of the most important decision of their lives, planned an expensive ceremony and reception, invited hundreds of guests, but had somehow never gotten around to asking, "What are we supposed to do when we get there?" When Mr. Emergency Clergy in Relief, probing a little further, asked the couple if they were (at least) ready to say their vows, they replied, "Isn't that what YOU do? Why don't you just say some things and then we'll do the 'I do' part. That should be good enough."

Do you look forward to the day when you will do the "'I do' part"? What exactly will you be agreeing to "I do" on that momentous day? In this study we're going to try something tricky. We're going to look at the idea of marriage in a way that, I hope, will both sober and envision you to prepare yourself for the day when the great "I do" tumbles out of your mouth.

---

1 Which of the following topics do you suspect you would find most helpful if it were to be covered in premarital counseling?

❑ How to handle your in-laws

❑ How to handle finances

❑ How to keep romance alive in a marriage

❑ How to receive correction from your spouse

❑ How to get rid of your spouse's cat

What Ever Happened to Happily Ever After?

Meditate on Hebrews 13:4. In what ways does our society dishonor marriage today?

First, let's affirm that we can no longer look to our culture for any clues regarding either the definition of a good marriage, or how to have one. One young woman summed up the marriage lessons she has absorbed from her parents' generation: "They now say that the first marriage is for love, the second is for money, and the third is for sex."[1]

This isn't to say Americans don't know how to throw a great wedding—the *average* cost of a wedding in the United States these days is just under $20,000! Folks are also bringing considerable creativity into their wedding plans. Skydiving weddings, scuba-diving weddings, and other oddities have become almost commonplace. Disney World has even gotten in on the deal, offering the "Ultimate Fairy Tale Wedding," which includes a Cinderella gown and glass coach for the princess/bride, a white horse for the prince/groom, an exclusive party in the Magic Kingdom, and the wedding night in a honeymoon castle. All this at the bargain price of $100,000.

And what of the enchanted couples enjoying such fairytale experiences? Unless they have something more unifying than a lot of spare cash, chances are that only about half will be able to live "happily ever after."

It's not that people don't want marriage to work. The number of marriage counselors jumped from 1,000 in 1972 to more than 50,000 in 1998, yet divorce rates have remained at about 50 percent for years. Marriage failure is now seen as a normal part of American life. A nationwide poll in the early 1990s showed that almost 60 percent believed it was best to draw up a prenuptial agreement before marriage[2]—in effect, a kind of a cross between a life insurance policy and a will, so if the marriage dies we can minimize all that unpleasant squabbling as we divide the spoils.

> ❝ Marriage, it has been said, is like a besieged fortress. Everyone inside wants to get out, and everyone outside wants to get in.[3] ❞
> — **Ruthe Stein**

Let's face it. As a culture, we have become experts at weddings and failures at marriage.

I wish I could say God's church is a beacon of light in this confusion, but it is not. The failure rate of Christian marriages lags just barely behind that of the overall population. It appears many professing Christians have a very non-Christian view of marriage. I regularly get calls from people outside our church who want me to perform a Christian wedding ceremony but have no awareness of the basic biblical teaching on marriage. A guy once called me and said he needed me to perform a ceremony in two weeks. He said he and his fiancée were Christians. I told him I couldn't do it unless I was confident this marriage was being established on a biblical basis and I suggested that I meet with them first. He replied, "I'm sorry, I'd love to do things according to the Bible, but I've got all my rel-

Meditate on Proverbs 21:5. What kind of problems could be caused by a hasty decision to marry?

atives coming into town for a reunion, and it's cheaper to do it then than for us to wait and have them come back later." I hope it was a good reunion.

For most single people, marriage is at least a dream, and for some it is becoming a fast-approaching reality. For those who dream, a good dose of biblical reality will help you dream with purpose. For those who are in relationships where marriage is a real possibility, I'd like to help you think beyond dresses, guest lists, and china patterns. For those who have experienced the pain of divorce, an understanding of God's perspective on marriage may help you sort out the past and view the future with renewed hope and wisdom. So let's examine together the biblical view of marriage.

At the Heart: A Covenant

The Bible, both in its precepts and examples, has a great deal to say about marriage. Perhaps the most concentrated teaching on marriage is found in Paul's letter to the Ephesians. Paul addresses marriage in the middle of a discussion on the life of the church. If you haven't pondered this passage recently, take a moment to do so now.

For Further Study: Read Hebrews 8:6-13. What differences between the Old Covenant and the New Covenant do you find in this passage?

Submit to one another out of reverence for Christ. Wives, submit to your husbands as to the Lord. For the husband is the head of the wife as Christ is the head of the church, his body, of which he is the Savior. Now as the church submits to Christ, so also wives should submit to their husbands in everything. Husbands, love your wives, just as Christ loved the church and gave himself up for her to make her holy, cleansing her by the washing with water through the word, and to present her to himself as a radiant church, without stain or wrinkle or any other blemish, but holy and blameless. In this same way, husbands ought to love their wives as their own bodies. He who loves his wife loves himself. After all, no one ever hated his own body, but he feeds and cares for it, just as Christ does the church—for we are members of his body. "For this reason a man will leave his father and mother and be united to his wife, and the two will become one flesh." This is a profound mystery—but I am talking about Christ and the church. However, each one of you also must love his wife as he loves himself, and the wife must respect her husband (Eph 5:21-33).

For Further Study:
Read Hebrews 13:20-21. How do we know that the New Covenant has power to help us please God in marriage or any other work we are called to do?

There is a lot of rich, practical truth to be drawn from this passage, but don't miss the underlying theology. The institution of marriage is rooted in a deeper institution: the New Covenant of Christ with his body, the Church.

The theology of marriage is a covenant theology. In Study Seven we discussed the covenantal aspect of relationships. Covenant is the binding promise of fidelity at the heart of Christian marriage. Jesus' covenant with us allows us to enter into a meaningful marriage covenant with another: "We love because he first loved us" (1Jn 4:19). All the elements of a biblical marriage—roles and responsibilities, communication and conflict resolution, romance and intimacy, parenting, etc.—flow out of an understanding of covenant and are empowered by the grace that flows to us through our covenantal position as God's beloved children.

Covenant is at the heart of marriage, and wedding vows are at the heart of the marriage covenant. The only reason to even have a wedding ceremony is to commit yourselves to one another under God through vows. There is nothing symbolic or ceremonial about covenant vows. They must be taken seriously.

> **❝** Marriage is the most vulnerable state of human existence. Here is where we have the most to lose. Here is where we are absolutely open. Here commitment means everything....'How do I know when I am deeply enough in love to get married?'...'When you love that person enough to publicly commit yourself to him or her for the rest of your life.'[4] **❞**
>
> **— R.C. Sproul**

In the Bible we see a remarkable thing. People experience the great provision and kindness of God. Out of thankfulness they turn to him in praise and adoration. Out of this heartfelt worship come great vows of commitment and sanctification. In the Bible people are warned never to vow lightly and never to vow what they cannot fulfill (Ecc 5:4-5).

Vows are an expression of ultimate trust. They are not conditional promises: "I'll do this *if* you do that." A marriage vow is unilateral. It says, "I commit my life to this marriage and renounce my right to take my life back." Marriage is not a negotiated partnership—it is a total commitment of myself to another for the duration of my life. Many single men and women will perform the ritual of the wedding vow this year. I suppose nearly every person vowing marriage commitment sincerely desires to make it work. But as we know, statistics indicate half will fail to follow it through to the end.

For Further Study:
Read Genesis 28:10-22. What caused Jacob to make his vow at Bethel?

133

Meditate on Deuteronomy 23:21-23. Why are vows to God treated so seriously in the Bible?

You see, vows are not a wish list of what we would like to take place in our marriage. Nor are they the mumbo-jumbo of religious formality. Covenant vows are the blueprint that determines how a Christian marriage will be built. We should be willing to evaluate our marriage based on our vows, and have our contribution to the marriage evaluated by our vows. Marriage vows are unnervingly practical.

---

2 Which of the following promises would be good for wedding vows and which wouldn't?

Good	Not Good	
❏	❏	"I promise to be truthful to you"
❏	❏	"I promise to always think of you first"
❏	❏	"I promise to be what you want me to be"
❏	❏	"I promise to be your best friend"
❏	❏	"I promise you'll never have a cat"

Most of the couples I marry write their own vows, and I always insist they allow me to review their vows prior to the wedding. I do this to assure myself and them of two things: that the vows are consistent with biblical teaching on marriage, *and* that they can actually be kept. Don't vow "I will never be angry with you," because you'll probably break that one during the reception. "I will never leave you," however, is a perfectly "keepable" vow, and one all couples should include. The wise single man or woman will give thought to what he or she will vow *before* getting to the altar.

Meditate on Proverbs 20:25. How can you keep from being rash in what you dedicate yourself to?

Beyond covenant vows, the biblical theology of a marriage covenant has several other very practical implications. Let's take a look at a few that are rooted in the passage from Ephesians quoted at page 132.

Want to See My Wedding Pictures?

Who is the most influential person at a wedding? The bride? The groom? The mom? In my experience it is often the photographer. People pay a great deal of money to have a stranger intrude on their every intimate wedding moment, posing people like fruit in a still-life, all in the name of "preserving the memory of this day." When people tell you that on your wedding day you are treated like royalty, don't forget that the privilege includes being hounded by paparazzi.

> **Marriage is an exclusive heterosexual covenant between one man and one woman, ordained and sealed by God, preceded by a public leaving of parents, consummated in sexual union, issuing in a permanent mutually supportive partnership, and normally crowned by the gift of children.[5]**
>
> **— John Stott**

The photos, of course, are a great keepsake that will be treasured always. But what I'm leading up to here is the fact that marriage is itself a picture with the most profound and eternal implications. I refer to the picture you will show people *through* your marriage. For marriage is, as one commentator put it, "The highest earthly type [picture] of the grandest heavenly fact—namely, the mystical union of the eternal Word with his Bride, the Church."[6]

"For this reason a man will leave his father and mother and be united to his wife, and the two will become one flesh. This is a profound mystery—but I am talking about Christ and the church" (Eph 5:31-32). Paul's astounding claim is that marriage is for even greater things than companionship, family, heritage, or social stability. The greatest, grandest reason for marriage between man and woman is to display the eternal relationship between Christ and his Church!

For Further Study:
2 Corinthians 6:14-18. Why does the Bible prohibit Christians from marrying non-Christians?

How does this happen? It's no accident Paul quotes directly from Genesis 2:24, where God joins the first man and woman together. By quoting the Genesis passage, Paul is letting us know that *before sin even entered the world* God had a plan of salvation. It involved his Son coming in the flesh and gathering together a people to be his "Bride," Christ redeeming the unlovely through his own death so they might be beautiful companions throughout eternity. In Revelation 19:7-9 we actually get a preview of the greatest wedding video of all time—the marriage celebration of the Lamb of God to his pure and spotless Bride, the Church.

Marriage then, is not merely about romantic history. More importantly, it is about redemptive history. That is why the writer of Hebrews commands us that "Marriage should be honored by all" (Heb 13:4). Any adulteration of the biblical view of marriage distorts the redemptive picture God has developed. A marriage that conforms to the

THE GIFT OF SINGLENESS: A GIFT FOR THE AGES

Most of you reading this book will one day be married. But if you think your true contribution can't be made *unless* you are married, let me introduce you to some folks who lived their lives in the gift of singleness with great purpose and impact.

Do you believe there is a limit to how God can use you in ministry? If so, think of Francis Asbury, founder of American Methodism; Phillips Brooks, the best-known American preacher of the early 1900s; J. Gresham Machen, founder of Westminster Seminary; or Kenneth Scott Latourette, one of the greatest church historians of this century. How about Corrie Ten Boom? How about Audrey Wetherell Johnson, pioneer in modern personal devotional literature and founder of the Bible Study Fellowship; or Henrietta Mears, shaper of modern Christian education and a woman who had a thriving outreach to Hollywood show-business types! Don't forget C. S. Lewis, a single man for all but a few years of his long life. We wouldn't have *The Chronicles of Narnia* or *Mere Christianity* if this "confirmed bachelor" hadn't made such good use of his singleness.

Singles have always been at the forefront of the spread of the gospel. The first modern missionary, David Brainerd, was a single man who evangelized the Indians of New England in the 1700s. His diary inspired another great early missionary, single man Henry Martyn of England. The early 20th century was a time when the gospel was expanding into new lands at an unprecedented pace. In 1900 alone, Elanor Chestnut and Lottie Moon were serving in China, Mary Slessor was working in the villages of Africa, and Amy Carmichael was beginning to rescue girls from temple prostitution in the slums of India. They would be followed by Gladys Aylward, whose missionary heroism in China was chronicled in the film "The Inn of Sixth Happiness." All were single women.

"Jesus Loves Me, This I Know" (the simplest song of Christian worship) and "The Messiah" (the most majestic) were both written by life-long singles: Anna Barlett Warner wrote the former, while George Friedrich Handel penned his immortal "Messiah" in an inspired three weeks. Other singles who have contributed to the rich worship tradition of the church include Elizabeth Cecilia Clephane ("Beneath the Cross of Jesus"); Adelaide Addison Pollard ("Have Thine Own Way"); Frances Havergal ("Take My Life and Let it Be"); and George Matheson ("O Love That Will Not Let Me Go"). And of course single man Isaac Watts' pen contributed more than 600 hymns to the church.

R.C. Sproul lists four men whom he considers, after the Apostle Paul, the most important Christian theologians: Augustine, Thomas Aquinas, Martin Luther, and John Calvin. Being celibate priests, Augustine and Aquinas never married; Luther married at age 42; and Calvin was married just ten years before being widowed. As single men, these pillars of the church were used by God to shape not only the church but the history of the Western world.

The gift of singleness is not just a gift to the individual believer, it is a gift to the body of Christ, and always has been.

For Further Study:
Read Matthew 22:1-14.
What does the parable
of the wedding feast
tell us about who will
be in attendance at the
marriage supper of the
Lamb?

biblical pattern God has set will actually testify to the
greater reality of God's love for his people. I don't know
about you, but for me this goes way beyond mystery—this
is entering brain-frying realms.

Biblical teaching establishes an order for marriage that
is not arbitrary, but very purposeful—marriage is meant
to reflect the relationship between Christ and the Church.
This biblical order determines the way we approach the
role of husband or wife in a marriage. There is much con-
troversy about the issues of headship and submission in
the church today, and there is no way I can adequately
address all the issues involved in this discussion. The recommended resources at the end of this study can help you
sort out the issues. Perhaps an illustration, however, will
help shed light on the wisdom of God's order for roles in a
marriage.

> **❝** Headship is the divine calling to take
> primary responsibility for Christlike, servant
> leadership, protection, and provision in the
> home. Submission is the divine calling of a
> wife to honor and affirm her husband's
> leadership and help to carry it through
> according to her gifts.[7] **❞**
>
> — **John Piper**

Jill and I wanted to have
ballroom dancing at our
wedding reception. Since we
were going to be on display,
we thought we had better
learn some steps in advance.
We soon found that ball-
room dancing is the ulti-
mate team endeavor. Good
ballroom dancers function
in sync, and almost seem to
be moving as one—not
because they held a strategy session beforehand, but
because inherent in the dance are defined roles: leading
for the man, following for the woman. All the man's steps
are leading steps; all the woman's steps are following
steps.

For Further Study:
Read 1 Peter 2:25-3:7.
What is one reason
wives should exercise
submission to their
husbands? What is one
reason husbands
should respect their
wives?

We were cool with the program in theory, but soon discovered a problem. While Jill was picking things up easily,
I danced more like Fred Flintstone than Fred Astaire. I had
so much trouble with the steps and counts I couldn't even
begin to think about leading Jill. The obvious solution, I
thought, was to let Jill take up the slack and lead until I
got my dancing shoes working. But (besides being scolded
mercilessly by the dance instructor) Jill's efforts to lead
created major train wrecks. Her steps aren't designed as
leading steps and mine are not following steps. Instead of
an elegant picture of perfectly synchronized artistic
expression, the best we could muster was a fitful and con-
tentious shuffle around the fringe of the dance floor.

3 Write a one-sentence definition for the following terms:

Headship:

Submission:

Hairball (extra credit):

In some ways, ballroom dancing is a lot like marriage. Both have an order that cannot be compromised. Unless you just don't care about the results, each person must understand his or her roles and responsibilities and embrace them gracefully. When done well, the man's leadership allows the woman's beauty and unique gifts to flow freely. In turn, the woman's submission allows the man to set a pace and direction appropriate for the couple and the environment. Ballroom dancing, like marriage, is meant to display more than the sum of its parts. The beauty is in the teamwork, not the talent.

> **" I acknowledge the kind hand of the heavenly Father. In changing my name, he has allowed me to take the name of one who loves the cause of Christ, and makes the promotion of it the business of my life. One who is, in every respect, the most calculated to make me happy and useful, of all the persons I have ever seen.**[8] **"**
>
> **— Ann Hasseltine Judson, first American woman missionary, speaking of her husband**

Jill and I deeply appreciate the roles God has given us in our marriage. I am not naturally a take-charge guy, and can be passive in decision-making. Jill is very capable of leading in many areas, but would tend to be impulsive in her decisions. If we built our marriage according to our natural strengths and preferences, her assertiveness and my tendency to avoid responsibility would create constant battles. But, by God's grace, I have embraced my leadership responsibility and she has taken up a vision for submission. As a result, I have grown in making decisions, and Jill enjoys the freedom to express her initiative without fearing the consequences of ill-considered actions. We share the goal of presenting a clear and attractive view of marriage to the world, and it takes both of us functioning gladly in our God-ordained roles for that to happen.

I don't know of anyone who can think about marriage

Meditate on 1 Timothy 3:1-13. Why is the marriage of a Christian leader so important?

roles without experiencing some degree of apprehension. Certainly there are abuses in the way people have applied this important biblical teaching. But just remember: if your Father in heaven has called you to reflect the joy of redemption through the prism of marriage, he will divinely enable you to fulfill your role. And don't forget to enjoy the dance.

To Form a More Perfect Union

In Ephesians 5:31, Paul presents the two main steps of entering into a marriage relationship—we *leave* one state of life, and become *united* to another person for life. Let's examine these steps a little further.

Meditate on Genesis 2:18-25. In what ways did God establish marriage as the closest of human relationships?

For many single people, the idea of leaving home to get married just doesn't apply. If you haven't been under direct parental supervision for years, what is there to leave? But in this passage, the idea of leaving applies to far more than parents and a childhood home. Anyone who has lived the single life knows you develop some pretty strong habits. There is no one to tell you where to put your keys (or to get on your case when you can't find them). No one will be irritated when you're an hour late getting home. No one cares how bad you look when you get up in the morning, or even how long you stay that way.

But "leaving," as Paul uses the word, is not exclusively an issue of authority relationships, or even of geography. It's an issue of your heart and your habits. Marriage means leaving certain things at the altar. Forever.

> ❝ Marriage is death to privacy, independence, childhood's home and family, death to unilateral decisions and the notion that there is only one way of doing things, death to the self. When these little deaths are gladly and wholeheartedly accepted, new life—the glory of sacrificial love which leads to perfect union—is inevitable.[9] ❞
>
> — **Elisabeth Elliot**

In marriage, I *leave* my tendency to walk away from unresolved conflict. I *leave* the influence of those things and people that would pull me away from my beloved. I *leave* expectations that someone else must change for my benefit. I *leave* much of what I have built by myself. Ask most any newlywed couple what they left behind at the altar. The list will be long, interesting, and still growing.

The purpose for leaving is to join another person with whom you want to spend the rest of your life (and every-

For Further Study:
Read 1 Corinthians 7:1-
5. What is the danger
of having a marriage
where intimacy is not
maintained?

one said, "Amen!"). This is not about housemating. This is about a union—what some Bibles translate "cleaving." Cleaving means not only permanent attachment, but aggressive, ongoing pursuit of another person. Cleaving is where romance finds its appropriate expression in the ongoing wooing of the one to whom God has joined you in marriage. It is also where sanctification—the daily process of putting off sin and growing in holiness, by which we become ever more like Christ—enters the wedding picture. God gave me a wife not just to meet a desire but to help me change! Marriage is not simply about combining our strengths, it is about refining our weaknesses. Maybe another illustration will help.

I love to take my family to Colonial Williamsburg, a town that has been meticulously restored to its 18th century character. One of my favorite things to do in Williamsburg is watch the blacksmith. I am fascinated by the patient heating and hammering of raw metal into sturdy and effective tools. These tools are often made from vastly different types of metal. In the hands of a skilled and patient blacksmith, diverse materials can be joined into a seamless unity, creating a tool perfectly suited for its assigned task. The process is called tempering.

**Meditate on Luke
20:27-40.** How does
Jesus' teaching here
affect your view of mar-
riage?

For example, to make an ax head, a blacksmith combines the heavy strength of iron with the lighter and more flexible strength of steel to fashion an alloy that can withstand a regular pounding yet retain its sharp edge. Tempering requires an intimate knowledge of the materials being combined, and the skill to blend them in right proportion for maximum effectiveness. In a well-made ax head the heavy portion is entirely iron, providing weight and strength. The blade of the head is entirely steel, for easy sharpening. In the middle the metals are blended into an alloy that cannot separate. If the ax head has too much iron, it will never stay sharp. If it has too much steel it will break. The tempering skill of the blacksmith is crucial.

In any marriage of God's design, an ongoing tempering process takes place. Over time two unique individuals begin to function as one. But the tempering process is not kind to our sinful nature. God puts us with another person who has a unique, innate ability to expose all our carefully hidden sinfulness. A cynic once said, "All marriages are happy. It's the living together afterward that causes all the trouble." In entering into the covenant of marriage, two single people not only open themselves to the inevitable troubles of a shared life together, they choose to embrace those troubles as good and necessary!

They recognize that growth in holiness requires change, and change requires seeing your sinful tendencies, and working in obedience to God to overcome them.

Jill and I have seen this tempering process at work in our life together. As you may have gathered, I am a low-gear person; I only go at top speed when necessary. Jill is a high-gear person; she will only down-shift when she has to. In the early years of our marriage, this produced a lot of fender-benders. But as we have grown in our union and dealt with the sin issues underlying our tendencies, we have learned to go at the same pace. Among other things, I am more efficient, and she is more at rest. Our marriage union is becoming a tempered union.

> **“** I have no doubt that where there is much love there will be much to love, and where love is scant faults will be plentiful. If there is only one good wife in England, I am the man who put the ring on her finger, and long may she wear it! God bless the dear soul! If she can put up with me, she shall never be put down by me.[10] **”**
>
> — **Charles Spurgeon**

4 We need to recognize that our spouse may not change easily in certain areas. Which of the following would you find difficult to accommodate in a spouse?

❑ Messiness   ❑ Driven-ness   ❑ Moodiness

❑ Forgetfulness   ❑ Cat allergies

For Further Study:
Read Malachi 2:13-16. How does the idea of divorce go against God's covenant nature?

Christian marriage is about spiritual growth—becoming more like Christ. God will not bring you together with someone just to answer your prayers or meet your needs. He brings people together in marriage to edify one another, to give them opportunity to lay down their lives for one another, to build a union designed primarily to bring glory to God. Anything that falls short of union falls short of God's plan. In marriage there can be no reluctant truces, no cold war, no "irreconcilable differences." But for any married couple desiring God's best, the tempering process is an adventure not to be missed.

Companions for Life

I wouldn't want to leave anyone with the impression that marriage is just slightly better than boot camp. As a pastor of single men and women of God, my greatest joy is to see two people come together in engagement for marriage. Why? Because the Scriptures give such a rich vision for the possibilities of marriage, and because time and again I've seen that vision come true. My own experience has made me the world's greatest booster for marriage.

When I look at my four precious children, I realize the joys I have as a father would not be possible but for my marriage. When I think of who I am as a Christian man, I realize I would be so much less if not for the encouragement and example of my wife's strong faith. When I see how Jill and I have been able to serve together in ministry, I am amazed at the fruit that has emerged from our little partnership. But far more than anything, I am humbly, profoundly, and constantly grateful that God has given me a companion for life.

---

5 Which of the following best describes how parenting fits into your vision for marriage right now?

❏ I'll marry anybody who'll give me children

❏ I want the whole package—spouse and kids

❏ Once I get the marriage thing going, then I'll think about kids

❏ I'd rather get a cat

Meditate on Revelation 19:6-10. How often do you ponder the eventual wedding feast of heaven?

I realize that for some of you it may not be easy in this season of your life to rejoice with me. Some single people I know so idolize the hope of marriage that they believe nothing else can bring fulfillment. Others so fear marriage that they live in virtual denial of the possibility. Some singles seem to career between the two. Can I offer some counsel? While a few of you will never marry, the great majority will. For most of us the question is not whether we will marry, but will we marry well? Now is the time to prepare yourself to fulfill a God-given role in your future marriage. It is also the time to place your attention on the Lord and his perfect plan and timing.

Does this sound like contradictory advice? Maybe in one sense it is, but it is sound nonetheless. The same God who says it is a good thing to be single says it is a good thing to desire marriage (1Co 7:8, Pr 18:22). The same God who says "abandon all for the Kingdom" says he will provide all your needs (Mt 6:33). The same God who says "be content in all things" says "make your requests known to God" (Php 4:4-13). Do you trust him with your desire to be married, or with your fear of marriage? Remember, God is a covenant God. He doesn't forget his promises or his children. And the God who is the Covenant Maker is also the Covenant Keeper. He will keep that which is entrusted to his care.

> *Love as distinct from 'being in love' is not merely a feeling. It is a deep unity, maintained by the will and deliberately strengthened by habit; reinforced (in Christian marriages) by the grace which both partners ask, and receive, from God....'Being in love' first moved them to promise fidelity; this quieter love enables them to keep the promise. It is on this love that the engine of marriage is run: being in love was the explosion that started it.[11]*
>
> **— C.S. Lewis**

I hope this study has both sobered your expectations and renewed your zeal for the biblical vision of marriage. This vision is beautifully captured by the words of an old English Puritan pastor, Richard Baxter. Let me leave you with his perspective, which summarizes all I have just shared in a brilliantly simple way.

> The common duty of husband and wife is, entirely to love each other....and avoid all things that tend to quench your love....Especially to be helpers of each other's salvation: to stir up each other to faith, love, and obedience, and good works: to warn and help each other against sin, and all temptations; to join in God's worship in the family, and in private: to prepare each other for the approach of death, and comfort each other in the hopes of eternal life....To help one another bear their burdens...to be delightful companions in holy love, and heavenly hopes and duties, when all other outward comforts fail.[12] ∎

GROUP DISCUSSION

1. What would you like to be communicated through your wedding ceremony to those in attendance?

2. What do you notice most at a wedding or reception?

3. Suggest some possible reasons why the divorce rate

among Christians is almost as high as that of the overall population.

4. Who has had the greatest impact (positive or negative) on your view of marriage roles? What things do you believe about marriage because of that impact? Are those things true?

5. As you consider the idea of marriage, what is your greatest fear?

6. What are some things or habits (or pets) you know you would not be able to bring into a marriage?

7. What type of person would probably best help you to overcome those areas in which you sin most easily? How does this compare with the type of person you are attracted to?

8. What is most important to you about a future spouse?

9. How does your view of marriage affect your life and relationships at present? Are there any ways in which this view plays too important a role?

RECOMMENDED READING

The Intimate Marriage by R.C. Sproul (Minneapolis, MN: Bethany Fellowship, 1975)

Marriage, Divorce and Remarriage in the Bible by Jay E. Adams (Phillipsburg, NJ: Presbyterian and Reformed, 1986)

Your Family, God's Way by Wayne A. Mack (Phillipsburg, NJ: Presbyterian and Reformed, 1991)

ANSWER to Warm-Up
(from page 129): Believe it or not, the only one that is not a traditional wedding gift is (2), rubber. Nylon is for year number four, plastic is for year one, and tin is for year ten. Velcro has yet to make the list.

STUDY NINE
RICH IN HOPE

Strategy: The single life confronts the universal challenge of loneliness with biblical hope.

BIBLE STUDY Ephesians 1:18-19

WARM-UP Among Christians who see solitude as the highest form of holiness, some of the more radical were the Stylites of the fifth century. They were known as the Stylites because:

1. They dressed only in black to protest the styles of dress of the day.

2. They lived by themselves perched on high poles, copying their founder, Simon Stylitus.

3. They never bathed, so they were forced out of cities to live in huts known as styles, from which we get the word "sty."

4. In public they only sang, and never spoke. To try to win converts they traveled in four-man singing groups. This tradition was revived briefly in the early 1970s by a group known as the Stylistics.

(See page 159 for answer)

PERSONAL STUDY He spent most of his life afflicted by illnesses that made it difficult for him to engage in even the most mundane social interaction. As an adult he was barely five feet tall, and profoundly unattractive. His only opportunity for marriage came about through a pen-pal relationship with a woman whom he had never met. He proposed through the heartfelt words of a poetic letter. She accepted his proposal, but on their first meeting, one glimpse of the little fellow crushed her desire for their marriage. He never came close to marriage again. What feelings of rejection and loneliness must have swept over this man as he surveyed his life?

**Meditate on Proverbs
14:10.** Do you ever
think that some people
don't struggle with lone-
liness?

Loneliness. It's the unwelcome hitchhiker on the road
of singleness. Whether it enters through broken or unful-
filling relationships, lack of family connections, or transitory life situations, loneliness seems to invade our hearts
at inconvenient and vulnerable times. It has been clinical-
ly described as "an intensely painful sense of exclusion, of
rejection, of not mattering to anyone, and of being worthless."[1] The man described above knew it well. We will
return to his story later in this study.

Margaret Clarkson shares her experience of loneliness
as a single woman this way:

> There are times when such a depth of loneliness wells
> up within us, such a sense of alienation engulfs us,
> that we cry out to God in anguish at the apparent
> waste of His endowments. Rich personalities that
> know no blending with
> another; brilliant
> minds that know no
> kinship; full hearts that
> find no union with
> their kind—to what
> purpose is such waste?[3]

> **" If I'm such a legend, why am I
> so lonely?[2] "**
>
> — **Judy Garland**

It is this very sense of wastefulness that this book is
meant to address. I have sought in these pages to present
a robust and purposeful view of singleness. To that end, I
have endeavored to set before you a compelling vision—
for identity, character, impact, relationships, even for
marriage. I hope your perspective on this time in your life
has been affected for the better. But even if I have suc-
ceeded beyond my wildest dreams, there will still be occasional seasons where you experience the consuming cloud
of loneliness. Is loneliness the radioactive waste-product
of the single life that can't be disposed of or recycled? Or
is there some purpose, even hope, in loneliness from the
hand of our loving Father?

For Further Study:
Read John 16:29-33.
Why did Jesus tell his
disciples they would
desert him?

Darkness on the Edge of Town

One of the first things we need to realize is that loneliness, no matter how unique we perceive it to be, is a universal challenge. Mother Theresa called loneliness the leprosy
of the modern world.[4] Feelings of loneliness occur when
fallen human beings wrestle with the complexities of life.

While in college I was involved in a relationship that I
thought and hoped would lead to marriage. When she

broke off the romance, I was devastated. Having no relationship with Christ, I didn't know where to turn. I remember sitting alone in my dorm room for hours, listening over and over again to Bruce Springsteen's, "Darkness on the Edge of Town." The song is about an outcast who traveled in the shadows, away from the light of human connection. For a time, that outcast was me. My friends tried to cheer me up, but for a season of my life I was enveloped in the shadows of loneliness.

---

1 Write down the title of a song, book, film, or other work that has spoken to you during a time of loneliness.

For Further Study:
Read 1 Kings 19. In what ways did God respond to Elijah's complaint that he was the only follower of God left?

We will all go through seasons and events no one else can share. The death of a loved one, rejection in relationship, personal failure—these will always be lonely times. But loneliness is not always associated with isolation. Some of the most acute feelings of loneliness occur in the context of healthy relationships, including marriage. One reason marriage is addressed in this book is so that you will be prepared to become a companion in life—one who brings comfort to another, not one who contributes to loneliness.

The Bible presents several godly people whose lives included deep loneliness. As an outlaw hiding in a cave, David declared, "I have no refuge, no one cares for my life" (Ps 142:4). God's servant Job laments, "All my intimate friends detest me; those I love have turned against me" (Job 19:19). Naomi, upon losing her family and finding herself destitute and alone, cries, "Don't call me Naomi [pleasant]... Call me Mara [bitter] because the Almighty has made my

> **"** As the deer pants for streams of water, so my soul pants for you, O God. My soul thirsts for God, for the living God. When can I go and meet with God? My tears have been my food day and night, while men say to me all day long, 'Where is your God?' These things I remember as I pour out my soul: how I used to go with the multitude, leading the procession to the house of God, with shouts of joy and thanksgiving among the festive throng. Why are you downcast, O my soul? Why so disturbed within me? Put your hope in God, for I will yet praise him, my Savior and my God. **"**
>
> — **Psalm 42:1-6**

**Meditate on
Ephesians 4:22-24.**
Can you list some spe-
cific ways in which, this
week, you sought to put
off the old self and put
on the new?

life very bitter. I went away full but the Lord has brought
me back empty" (Ru 1:20). Like some of you, these saints
struggled with profound loneliness in the midst of unex-
pected and difficult circumstances. They struggled righ-
teously, but they struggled just the same.

Investing in Loneliness

Like the young man described at the beginning of this
study, often the circumstances fostering our loneliness
are not of our own creation. So what do we contribute to
our loneliness—nothing? No, we contribute plenty. We
talk as if we want to connect with others, but our hearts
betray us. At the heart of us (you, me, and everybody else)
is a heart of sin, and at the heart of sin is separation, primarily from God, and secondarily from one another. How
does sin provoke loneliness?

Loneliness can be made worse by **self-centeredness**—
the drive to arrange people and situations in orbit around
us. J. Oswald Sanders notes, "Without the aid of self-centeredness, loneliness would find it difficult to exist."[5] We
discussed the self-centered view of life, and the damage it
does to our relationship to God and others, in Study Two.
Self-centeredness always bears the fruit of loneliness.

Loneliness can also result from our **demanding will**.
Why do our relationships never seem as satisfying or beneficial as the relationships we perceive around us? Why do
we lack the patience to let relationships deepen through
trust and time? Why do we have so little grace for the
relational failures of others? I believe it's because the idols
of our hearts are both demanding and relentless.

For Further Study:
Read Luke 6:30-36. Is
it OK to demand justice
from someone who
wrongs you?

The Apostle James questions us, "What causes fights
and quarrels among you? Don't they come from your
desires that battle within you?" (Jas 4:1). James reveals
that it is not outward events, but my inward desires (that I
have elevated to the level of idolatrous demands) that lead
to relational breakdown. As we learned in Study Six, when
we begin to sacrifice relationships on the altar of our selfish demands, we destroy true fellowship. When this happens we experience the opposite of fellowship—loneliness.

In this maelstrom of sinful propensities and circum-
stantial challenges, where does God come into the picture? Charles Spurgeon reminds us,

God is all eye and all ear, and all his eye and all his
ear are for his people. Are you distressed in heart?
God sees your distress. Are you crying in secret in

148

the bitterness of your soul? God hears your cry. You are not alone. O lonely spirit, broken spirit, be not dismayed; be not given to despair. God is with you. If he sees nothing else, he will see you. "The eyes of the Lord are upon the righteous." And if he hears no one else in the world, he will hear you. "His ears are open to their cry."[6]

---

2 Psalm 68:6 states, "God sets the lonely in families." An alternate translation is, "God sets the desolate in a homeland." Using your own words, write another way of expressing this verse, based on your own understanding of and experience with God.

When I sense the darkness of loneliness encroaching, I try to remember Jesus, my Good Shepherd, the One who gathers his sheep to himself (including strays like me). He will lovingly discipline me in my sinfulness. He will identify with and comfort me in my distress. He will give me hope. And he will do no less for you. Regardless of the apparent reasons for our feelings of loneliness, we need to see them as the loving call of God; he desires us to draw close to him.

> **" ** What is God working on? Is He working hard to provide us with the biggest pile of this world's stuff and this world's happy experiences? If so, He has miserably failed. Even worse, He has used His creative and redemptive power to give us only that which is doomed to pass away. Would this be the work of a good God? Would a good God motivate us to hope in things that are by their very nature temporary?....Would He be good if He did anything less than to confront our powerful delusion of the permanence of this world?[7] **"**
>
> **— Paul Tripp**

God has great purposes in all manner of adversity, including all manner of loneliness. I would like to encourage you with two of these purposes: solitude and pilgrimage.

Solitude: Loneliness as a Discipline

Biblically defined, solitude is not isolation. It is opportunity for private communion with the Father. Elisabeth Elliot, a woman greatly acquainted with loneliness, talks about turning "your loneliness into solitude."[8] God employs solitude to form two qualities in us:

Holiness, a divine set-apartness; and

Stillness, a heart secure and devoted to God.

These qualities, so crucial for the Christian who wishes to serve God in this life, *cannot* be attained without the experience of solitude. When you encounter loneliness or a season of isolation, embrace your aloneness as solitude. God himself may have brought you to this point to meet with you.

My children's first pet was a cat named Nikko. As a kitten, Nikko would tend to get worked up by the bustle of the house. In this wired state he'd often rampage through the kids' games, homeschool areas, etc., attacking anything that moved. My children's solution was to banish him to the bathroom for some chill-out time. When he was eventually released, Nikko's disposition, while not exactly contrite, was much more feline than frantic. The change had been wrought through solitude.

Like Nikko, in my immaturity I can get all wound up by the bustle of life and cares of the world, even to damaging extremes. I'm so thankful that at those times the Lord graciously separates me to himself—so that I can once again be and act more like his child and less like his indispensable right-hand man.

---

3 In which of the following situations would you feel most lonely in a crowd?

❏ A wedding reception for a couple you barely know

❏ Waiting to catch a plane in a city you have never visited

❏ An area where you are a racial or ethnic minority

❏ A new church or small group

It is also helpful to remember that God brings us into solitude not so much to test us as to prepare us. Jesus himself experienced intense loneliness during his time on earth. Luke 4:1-14 records that Jesus was led by the Spirit

For Further Study:
Read Mark 6:30-34.
Did Jesus have to have
his "personal space"?

**Meditate on John 5:1-
8.** Reflect on the chal-
lenges of loneliness for
people who are physi-
cally handicapped.

into the wilderness. The isolation and temptation he experienced during that time did not weaken or compromise
his authority, they defined it. When he returned 40 days
later "in the *power* of the Spirit" his impact and ministry
began at once to be felt. In the wilderness, Jesus
exchanged earthly glory for heavenly glory.

As necessary as that 40 days of solitude was to the success of Jesus' ministry, it was not sufficient. Frequent,
shorter periods of solitude were a regular part of Jesus'
communion with his heavenly Father. He regularly drew
away from the crowds of mission and ministry for solitary
times of prayer. In the solitude of Gethsemane (Mt 26:36-
46), when even those with good intentions failed him,
Jesus found renewed strength and faith to face his crucifixion. Jesus submitted to the will of his Father and
exchanged "My will for Thy will," ultimately to be proven
in the Cross, the most intense loneliness ever experienced.

The Scriptures are full of saints (Moses, David, Elijah,
Paul, and others) whose "my will for thy will" exchange
occurred through times of prolonged solitude or relational poverty. Church history, likewise, is replete with testimony to the preparatory effect of solitude. Imprisoned for
more than twelve years for preaching the gospel, Puritan
John Bunyan wrote, "I never had in all my life so great an
inlet into the Word of God as now....Jesus Christ also was
never more real and apparent than now; here I have seen
and felt Him indeed."[9] It was in the solitude of prison that
he began to write "Pilgrim's Progress."

Missionary pioneer Hudson Taylor and the great evan-
gelist D. L. Moody both experienced failure that brought
intense loneliness and isola-
tion. Amy Carmichael lived
the last 20 years of her life
virtually confined to one
room because of illness. But
by turning these times of
isolation into times of solitude, these saints and
countless others like them
produced fruit that has
pushed the gospel forward
and inspired many discour-
aged souls. If you find yourself separated from the relationships that satisfy your soul, maybe God himself has
brought you to a time of preparation through solitude, a
time when all your satisfaction can be in him.

> ❝ It is a noble and a lofty spectacle to
> see amidst a race of frivolous mortals a
> soul, which being immortal, is intent upon
> its immortality, and though surrounded by
> the frivolities of this visible world, is intent
> upon the realities of the unseen
> state.[10] ❞
>
> — **John Angell James**

The Way of Hope

For Further Study:
Read Psalm 39:4-7.
When we realize how
short life is, what do
we look for?

"But I'm not Amy Carmichael, or D. L. Moody, or Hudson Taylor. I'm just me and all I feel I'm good for is filling a church seat and digging ruts I can't climb out of!"

Is this where you live? Has the gnawing of doubt and discouragement eaten the heart out of your faith? Are you frustrated that your SELF stubbornly refuses to budge from the driver's seat of your life? Have you quietly given up on dreams that once ignited your passion for God? Where do you turn when you've tried all the tricks and exhausted all the remedies for loneliness?

The Bible does give an answer: Hope.

Now, if you are like me, you tend to look at hope as sort of the Santa Claus of Christian virtues—good for setting a happy mood but not likely to deliver the goods on the big day. In our modern, comfortable Christianity, hope has taken a bad rap as the uncoordinated cousin of faith and love in the backyard football game of life. You know, "Faith will be the quarterback, Love can be the receiver, and Hope...um, you can hike the ball."

But in the Bible, hope stands triumphantly on its own. In fact, Paul tells the Colossians that faith and love actually spring from hope (Col 1:5). The hope of the Bible is energetic (a "living hope" in 1 Peter 1:3) and rock solid, an anchor for our souls both firm and secure (Heb 6:19). Hope doesn't simply stand pat, it compels us onward and upward—toward joy (Ro 12:12), peace (Ro 15:13), boldness (2Co 3:12), endurance (1Th 1:3), action (1Pe 1:13), and holiness (1Jn 3:3).

---

4 Commiting which of these social stumbles would, for you, be most likely to create a sense of isolation?

❑ Declaring an unpopular political opinion

❑ Talking approvingly of a movie that you suddenly realize others find objectionable

❑ Being the object of a practical joke

❑ Being offered a breath mint for no apparent reason

What is hope? *Essentially, hope is the ability given to us by God to view life from an eternal perspective.* Hope allows us to live in this oppressive and soul-numbing present world with spirits unbroken.

For Further Study:
Read Romans 5:1-5
(reproduced in the box
on this page). Why
doesn't hope disap-
point us?

How does it work? Hope emerges within us when we trust in the sovereignty and goodness of God. God's gift of hope is there for us at each moment—when life is pleasant and faith is strong and untested, but also (and even especially) when we face difficult circumstances with a battered faith.

The book of Lamentations tells the ghastly tale of the destruction of a civilization. The people about whom this book was written have rejected God and are reaping the horrible consequences of rebellion. Famine, disease, and devastation were the life experience of an entire generation. Yet in the midst of this terrible tribulation, hope springs up like a flower in the rubble. Listen to the power of hope.

> I remember my affliction and my wandering, the bitterness and the gall. I well remember them, and my soul is downcast within me. Yet this I call to mind and therefore I have hope: Because of the LORD's great love we are not consumed, for his compassions never fail. They are new every morning; great is your faithfulness. I say to myself, "The LORD is my portion; therefore I will wait for him." The LORD is good to those whose hope is in him, to the one who seeks him; it is good to wait quietly for the salvation of the LORD (La 3:19-26).

The Lamenter has known nothing but hardship in experience, yet he grasps on to the anchor of deeper truth—that "his compassions never fail." In other words, only God can promise good and deliver it without fail. This is where the power of hope ignites. It sees beyond present reality to the goodness and sovereignty of God, and it acts on that reality.

For the Christian, the greatest expression of God's sovereign goodness occurred in the death and resurrection of Jesus Christ. Therefore, *all Christian hope draws its authority from the resurrection of Christ*. Without the resurrection there is no reason to hope (1Co 15:19). Why?

> **"** Therefore, since we have been justified through faith, we have peace with God through our Lord Jesus Christ, through whom we have gained access by faith into this grace in which we now stand. And we rejoice in the hope of the glory of God. Not only so, but we also rejoice in our sufferings, because we know that suffering produces perseverance; perseverance, character; and character, hope. And hope does not disappoint us, because God has poured out his love into our hearts by the Holy Spirit, whom he has given us.[11] **"**
>
> — **Paul the Apostle**

JOY IN THE JOURNEY

There is a joy in the journey
There's a light we can love on the way
There is a wonder and wildness to life
And freedom for those who obey

And all those who seek it shall find it
A pardon for all who believe
Hope for the hopeless and sight for the blind

To all who've been born of the Spirit
And who share incarnation with Him
Who belong to eternity stranded in time
And weary of struggling with sin

Forget not the hope that's before you
And never stop counting the cost
Remember the hopelessness when you were lost

There is a joy in the journey
There's a light we can love on the way
There is a wonder and wildness to life
And freedom for those who obey

— Michael Card, 1986,
Birdwing Music/Mole End Music (ASCAP)

154

**Meditate on
1 Corinthians 15:13-
26.** How can this pas-
sage help you respond
to someone who says
it's OK to believe that
Jesus was a good man
but not God's son?

Because the resurrection not only authenticates the past compassion of God toward us, it guarantees that our future lies in life everlasting. Hope, remember, is *eternal perspective*. It searches out the deeper truth of existence and finds true and eternally valid reasons for faith in the present.

John Calvin describes this dynamic of faith and hope so clearly:

> Faith believes that God is true; hope expects that in due season he will manifest his truth. Faith believes that he is our Father; hope expects that he will always act the part of a Father towards us. Faith believes that eternal life has been given to us; hope expects that it will one day be revealed. Faith is the foundation on which hope rests; hope nourishes and sustains faith....Hope is nothing else than the food and strength of faith.[12]

Remember in Study One when we talked about the inadequacy of coping? Coping with life in general, and singleness in particular, is the opposite of hope. Coping is hopeless acceptance of "the hand you've been dealt." If there is one thing I want to communicate through this book, it's this—**a rich life, single or otherwise, is a life lived for the glory of God.** Hope always glorifies God, because it is a foretaste of the eternal life that he has given us. It is the lamp of welcome on our pathway home.

For Further Study:
Read Titus 2:11-14.
How should we live, as
we await our eternal
hope?

Of Refugees and Pilgrims

In 1994, one of the great tragedies of the 20th century occurred in the African country of Rwanda. An ethnic civil war triggered the genocidal massacre of more than 500,000 people in just a few short months. Hundreds of thousands of Rwandans fled to neighboring countries for asylum, creating instant refugee camps the size of cities. Many people died in the camps from disease, malnutrition, and further violence before some semblance of order was brought by international relief organizations.

Many of the refugees were children, orphaned when their parents died in the genocide. Others had simply gotten lost in the mass exodus of the refugees—cut off from their parents by the fleeing mob. Many children who made it to the camps were sent away by their sick parents to find a relief station, where "orphans" had a much better chance of receiving help than did children who arrived with parents. Temporary orphanages were built and filled overnight, but more orphans continued to pour across the borders.

A small but significant miracle occurred in one of these orphanages. A young, anonymous child had found a refuge from the chaos. Just a few months earlier, this child would have been growing up innocently in a small village. Now the child was alone and adrift in a violent world. But in the midst of that colossal nightmare, this lost child experienced a miracle. How do we know? A Christian relief worker came across the lyrics to a song, scribbled on a piece of scrap paper in the labored scrawl of a little child. It is a song that must have been sung through tears of despair and fear, a song of hope from within the midst of a hopeless situation.

> **"** They say that love can heal the broken
> They say that hope can make you see
> They say that faith can find a savior
> If you would follow and believe
> With faith like a child[13] **"**
>
> — **Dan Haseltine**

> I hear talking about the Heavenly home
> They tell me there are many houses
> They tell me that it is a very good place
> And it is very good to be there
> What wonderful country in which God lives!
>
> They tell me that my house is also there
> in that Heavenly home
> I hear that many friends are there
> that they are waiting for me in heaven
> Where the water of life is transparent and it comes
> from the throne of the King, God
>
> They tell me that Jesus is the King of that place
> I will see Him face to face when I reach there
> No lamentation will be there
> There will be peace in that house which is built in gold
>
> They tell me there will be no crying
> Jesus will take away tears from our eyes
> There is no sadness and there is peace in Heaven
> And a lot of enjoyment only[14]

This child was a homeless orphan, a refugee. But somehow in this lonely, desperate, hopeless chaos, hope broke through. A refugee became a pilgrim. That was the miracle.

What is a pilgrim? According to the dictionary, a pilgrim is one who travels in search of a sacred place, or a sojourner for reasons of faith. By contrast, a refugee survives. A refugee has no place to go.

A refugee can only cope.

Meditate on Psalm 84. Meditate on this Psalm as an itinerary for your personal pilgrimage in God.

But pilgrims are people on the move. We can't stop, won't stop—a goal awaits. So we live with purpose, with vision, and with wise investment of our lives. Are you a refugee...or a pilgrim? What this anonymous orphan child found, and what we in our own way need to grasp, is that the difference between a refugee and a pilgrim is hope— the blessed hope of Christ in you, the hope of glory. If you know Christ, you have hope, and you *are* a pilgrim.

Brothers and sisters, I have wanted this book to encourage you. It is meant to help you look at your singleness with greater joy and anticipation. I trust that reading it will challenge you to better use of your glorious opportunity as a single man or woman to exercise undivided devotion to the Lord. I pray that it will help you make better decisions and build better friendships, and that it will help you prepare for your call as a single—and for marriage, should that time come. But more than anything I want to inspire you to embrace the pilgrimage of the Christian life. I want you to be rich in hope.

---

5 Which of the following gives you the greatest sense of eternity?

❑ Times of worship

❑ Seeing someone come to Christ

❑ Answered prayer

❑ Experiencing the wonders of God's creation

Meditate on 1 Peter 1:3-7. How is hope presently living in your life?

To be a pilgrim means to embrace the challenges of life, and the loneliness of our singular journey, as investments in hope. A. W. Tozer once wrote: "Most of the world's great souls have been lonely. Loneliness seems to be the one price the saint must pay for his saintliness."[15] Beyond seasons of solitude, there is an abiding loneliness that all who walk the path of Christ must embrace—singles and marrieds alike. Though often hidden in the fabric of our busy

> **❝** Home is where our Father is. While we are content to be on our Father's business here in these seventy-year motel rooms we call bodies, we are never entirely at home. How can we be? Our true home is so far superior, and the spiritual family there so vast and rich. The Great Reunion awaits us, and we long for it.[16] **❞**
>
> **— Randy Alcorn**

lives, the loneliness of pilgrimage is familiar to us all.

But the cost of this pilgrimage is nothing compared to the riches to be enjoyed at the end of the journey. It is like trading play money for bars of pure gold. Many have walked the road before you and are now waiting to cheer you to the finish (Heb 11). Some of them you have encountered in this book. Others will walk alongside you on the way as dear traveling companions. God may even give you one person to be your lifelong partner in pilgrimage. No matter what your future on this earth holds, at this moment you are a single person walking a pilgrimage in the gift of singleness. Do it for the glory of God.

And when you get to the end, *he* will be there. The Blessed Hope with arms outstretched and a big smile on his face. He has prepared a place for you, a city, a house, a place at his table. And at that table there will be an exchange—your loneliness for rest, your suffering for glory, the perishable for the imperishable, pilgrimage for home. The Rich Single Life will have been lived, and the eternal inheritance which has been kept in heaven for you, will be yours!

* * * * * * *

By the way, whatever happened to the poor little pilgrim at the beginning of this study? His name was Isaac Watts, and though he remained single all his life, he too found hope in his journey. From this hope came more than 600 hymns to the glory and faithfulness of God, including these words of encouragement to the lonely pilgrim:

O God our Help in ages past,
Our hope for years to come
Be Thou our Guide while life shall last,
And our eternal home.[17] ∎

1. Make a list of words that describe the experience of loneliness

2. What kinds of everyday experiences can trigger feelings of loneliness for you?

ANSWER to Warm-up
(from page 145):
If your fifth-century history is a little rusty, the correct answer is (2).

3. What can cause loneliness in a marriage relationship? What can help prevent it?

4. How does self-centeredness tend to express itself in you?

5. How can you know when your expectations of a relationship are appropriate and when they are demanding?

6. Describe a time when you realized that God was at work separating you to himself.

7. Why do we as Christians have such trouble when faced with a "my will or thy will" decision? (See p. 151)

8. When faced with loneliness, where are you likely to turn?

9. Describe a time when you found hope in God.

10. How can you keep from coping and start hoping?

RECOMMENDED READING

Future Grace by John Piper (Sisters, OR: Multnomah Books, 1995)

Facing Loneliness by J. Oswald Sanders (Grand Rapids, MI: Discovery House, 1990)

Loneliness by Elisabeth Elliot (New York, NY: Fleming H. Revell, 1989)

Single Parents and the Church

In a culture characterized by disintegration of the family, churches are a strong fortress for the defense of healthy nuclear (two-parent) families. Also, churches are increasingly aware that single adults are a wonderful resource for the ministry and vitality of the church. In between two-parent families and single adults, however, lies a big gap. Into this gap fall single parents and their children. That gap—one of the greatest challenges facing the church in America—has several dimensions.

Identity. A single parent wrestles every day with a basic identity problem. Am I a single person who has parenting responsibilities? Or am I a parent who basically lives in a single person's world? It's tough to be both all the time.

Many of the single parents I know seek their fellowship in our singles ministry, but find it challenging to flow in the spontaneous social realm of other singles. Singles often have very little understanding of the pressures of parenting, and may prefer to not even deal with children in their world of singleness.

Other single parents seek identity with two-parent families in a parents' world. This can provide a great environment of security and training for the children...but then the couples go home, and instantly the singleness of single parenting once again fills the void.

Values. Single parents are single for a variety of reasons, some of which are more "acceptable" than others. The widowed mother is a hero; the divorced father may not be. A never-married single mother may be honored for refusing an abortion, yet sense the ongoing doubts of others about her virtue. Many of us value stay-at-home parenting and decry daycare, but what is a single parent to do when he or she must work outside the home in order to provide? We talk about the need to train children with godly diligence and consistency, yet single parents must often raise their children within a complicated and competing system of authorities and influences—often including the other birth parent, grandparents, counselors, courts, attorneys, schools, media, peers, and social service agencies! Perhaps most challenging, a single parent often lives with the constant awareness that his or her greatest human joy, that wonderful child, is inextricably linked to personal shame, pain, failure, or loss of vast proportions.

Finances. A friend of mine is trying to build a new church. When starting a church, one of your prayers is that God would bring in a foundation of families who will provide stability and a financial base for the ministry. Right off the bat, my friend had a problem. His church is in an urban area, and he began getting an influx of single parents responding to the hope held out in the gospel. So, rather than a church filled with financial contributors, he was pastoring folks who not only needed particular care as single parents, but who also had overwhelming financial needs. This challenge is not confined to urban communities. Single-parent families typically have constant, legitimate material needs, needs that aren't solved just by a bag of groceries or a check.

Vision. Single parents live with the dilemma of trying to provide for their children both materially and relationally. They also live daily in the fear of failing in both areas. Fatigue and the ongoing task of raising a child without the support of a spouse can keep personal vision and faith locked into the stifling confines of day-to-day living. Every future decision—vocation, education, ministry, where to live—is defined by the challenges of being a single parent. Even the potential for marriage takes on a unique twist. A single mom must look at any potential husband and evaluate whether he could also be a more-or-less instant father (and this, she recognizes, is a chilling prospect for many single men). Also, any single parent beginning to build a relationship with a possible future spouse must exercise the added care of assuring that his or her child does not begin to bond with this possible "new Mom/Dad" until there is some degree of certainty that wedding bells will, in fact, ring.

The Call to the Church

As we acknowledge the various dimensions of the single-parent gap, let us also recognize that God in his wisdom has provided an ideal place for single-parent families. It is the local church: a community of faith, the family of God.

The biblical equivalent of single parents are the widows and orphans of ancient times. In the Old Testament, God's people Israel were called to both provide for the widowed and fatherless and uphold their just cause (Dt 24; Ps

82:3). In the book of Acts, one of the first issues facing the new church was how to provide for widows and their children (Ac 6).

We who are the members of local churches need to welcome single parents and their children into our midst as fellow recipients of the mercy of God. Without creating unhelpful dependencies, we need to be willing to see their needs as legitimate and worthy of our long-term attention. We also must be prepared to stand with them in the legal system, the government-assistance system, and perhaps most importantly, in our own little social systems. We need to bend our way of doing things to include them and their children, and help them find their practical place in the church family.

The Call to the Single Parent

Another beautiful aspect of God's plan for the single parent is that, along with his provision, God issues a call. It is a call to trust and a call to act. Paul writes to Timothy concerning how to care for the single parents in his church:

> Give proper recognition to those widows who are really in need. But if a widow has children or grandchildren, these should learn first of all to put their religion into practice by caring for their own family and so repaying their parents and grandparents, for this is pleasing to God. The widow who is really in need and left all alone puts her hope in God and continues night and day to pray and to ask God for help (1Ti 5:3-5).

As single parents find a place in God's church, they should be cared for. This does not mean, however, that the church exists to fulfill the demands of its members (or any subset of its members). As the church cannot expect a single parent to bend fully to its ways, the single parent likewise cannot expect accommodation on every front. Instead, faith is expressed on both "sides." Such faith is first expressed through responsible sacrifice, and then in trusting God for what remains. One single mom expresses both the tension and blessing of accepting a vital role in her local church this way:

> Time is a precious commodity to a single parent, and giving so much of it in service is a definite sacrifice for my family. But I also know that it has con-

nected us closely to our church family. When I'm involved at church, my children not only see me modeling servanthood, but they also see many other people committed to the Lord and working together for his purposes. I thank God for these opportunities he's given me to serve. It's also a lot of fun! (*People of Destiny*, July/August 1995, p. 6)

Andrew Murray once wrote: "Abide in Christ and let your child feel that to be near you is to be near Christ." Don't disqualify yourself or your child from full participation in God's agenda for your times. There is a vital role for you to play.

Father to All

The overarching hope of the single parent is the Fatherhood of God. The psalmist expresses it this way,

Sing to God, sing praise to His name
Extol Him who rides on the clouds
His name is the Lord; rejoice before Him
A Father to the fatherless; A defender of widows
Is God in His holy dwelling (Ps 67:4-5)

Notice two things. God the Father has a special place in his heart for the widows and the fatherless. His great heart beats with compassion for those who are his and are going it alone. But he is the Father "in His holy dwelling." He is not only willing, but fully able in his sovereignty to meet the needs of his loved ones. How does he do it?

• He gives every one of his children a family large enough to fit in—the church.
• He answers prayer—every promise given to parents is available to the single mom or dad.
• He restores and protects. I have met so many single parents whose lives are a chaotic mess because of financial stress, poor choices, and isolation. And I have seen order and faith come to these seemingly hopeless situations as God's ways and means are embraced through faith.

But sometimes the most significant blessings from God are the smallest. One such small blessing occurred in a large conference that our church attends every year. During worship one evening, the worship leader, Bob Kauflin, sensed that the Lord wanted to minister specifically to the single parents in the gathering through a spontaneous song (not an infallible word from the Lord—only Scripture holds that place—but simply an expression of God's heart). Streams of people, men and women from across the spectrums of age and race, came forward to receive ministry. The song that emanated from that moment clearly touched the hearts of many, a number of whom began to weep with joy. For months afterward my single-parent friends were sharing with me how that immediate expression of God's specific care for them had changed their lives. The song was recorded and transcribed. I'd like to close with it as a reminder of how the God of all creation has kept a place in his heart just for single moms and dads.

> You've felt so many times this isn't what I planned
> Days of loneliness, nights of pain
> You've felt so many times you'd rather have it any
>   other way
> But I'm with you right now
> And I want you to know
> That my plans are greater than you'll ever know
>
> I am the one who's brought you to this place
> I am the one who will take you on
> You will know my strength in the heat of battle
> When there's no hand to hold on to
>
> You will know my strength when you feel like falling
> You will know my arms around you
> For my plan for you is perfect
> I've seen every detail of your life
>
> Yes my plan for you will never fail
> Though you've experienced so many wrongs in
>   your life
> Still, my plan for you is perfect
> And I will not let you down
>
> For my love for you remains this day
> I will see you through all the way!
> I will see you through all the way! ■

Divorce and the Redemptive Power of God

Samantha was nervous. She sat across the desk from a man she hardly knew, ready to spill her heart. The tale she told me that day was one of regrettable decisions and sorrowful consequences. It was deeply personal, but sadly familiar to a pastor's ears.

"Several years ago I met a guy at the gym where I worked out. He was good-looking and nice and we started dating. Eventually we moved in together. It was the logical thing to do. I wasn't a Christian at the time but I couldn't get over the awkwardness of the situation. I used to have nightmares of a surprise visit by my mother and would never be able to look the other tenants in the apartment building in the eye. I kept pressing Steve that we should get married, and I guess he finally ran out of excuses. It was an OK wedding, but the party at the reception was great.

"The first few months after that were fine, but we really didn't know what we were doing. We started arguing and he started staying out more with his buddies, which was fine with me. When he asked for the divorce I was hurt, but I wasn't shocked. After the divorce he went his way and I went mine, which was into counseling to find out how I had messed up my marriage. Being alone, I started thinking about God more and I eventually gave my life to Jesus at a Christian concert. I started going to a church. Everything was fine until I told them I was divorced.

"'I'm sorry,' they told me, 'but if you are divorced you're in sin and you can't be a member here until you get back with your husband.' Unfortunately, Steve had gotten remarried, so that wasn't a possibility. I kept visiting that church for a while, but I don't think they ever trusted me.

"When I started coming here I planned on not telling anybody I was divorced. I don't know what I'd do if another church rejected me. My family thinks I drove Steve away by nagging. All of my friends, I found out, were really his friends first. I don't need counseling, I need fellowship. I don't want to go back to the meat market. If I can't find a church that will accept me, I don't know where I'll turn. But I feel like I'm deceiving people

to pretend I've never been married. Basically I'm sitting here between a rock and a hard place. Either I act like somebody I'm not or I let people know who I am and risk being rejected again. So here's the issue—Can God love a divorced person? Can I find a church home here?"

I deeply respected Samantha's integrity and courage. I also realized this was a crucial moment. My response would fill the yawning gaps in her belief about the nature of God's love and forgiveness, the purpose of God's church, the authority of God's Word, and the meaning of her new life in Jesus. My response actually involved a series of discussions during the next several months, during which we worked through the challenges she faced as a divorced person trying to walk in obedience to Christ.

The following thoughts are essentially a summary of those interactions. Space does not permit a detailed discussion of all the scriptural issues regarding divorce. Godly leaders have taken different positions regarding the meaning of the relevant texts. The pastoral staff at my church has studied the issue and developed a policy on divorce and remarriage that is scripturally sound and supported by much of the recognized scholarship. It is also open to adjustment as we confront compelling arguments that do not concur. My purpose in this appendix is not to define the status of every divorced person, but to give hope and counsel about how a person who is "single by legal decree" can find meaningful connection to God's purpose and people.

The first thing I wanted Samantha to know was that the love of God did not find an insurmountable obstacle in the fact of divorce. Jesus held out the water of life to a Samaritan woman who had had five husbands (Jn 4:7-18). The first people who were given opportunity to respond to the good news of the death and resurrection of Jesus were those who crucified him (Ac 2:29-41). Samantha shared with me the wonderful testimony of her breaking and submission to Christ following her divorce. She needed to know that she was not "damaged goods" in God's house, or a second-class citizen in his kingdom. The sovereign God who works all things together for the good of those who love him (Ro 8:28) had put his love in her heart through the miracle of regeneration. I had the great privilege of presenting a cool drink of the mercy of God to a very thirsty refugee. She was now an adopted daughter of the King, and it was easy to welcome her into the family of our church.

With a trust of biblical acceptance established, we could begin to look at what God's word said about her experience. She was able to begin to see the lies she had adopted from the culture. She had been told in counseling that the divorce was nobody's fault—just the inevitable result of irreconcilable differences. Yet this didn't relieve the nagging sense of guilt for how she got into, or managed, or exited her marriage. Self-esteem was an untrusted support (it was never there when she needed it). When she began to see that divorce is a choice exercised by people who have devalued the marriage covenant and are grappling with deeper issues of sin, she found a reason for her perpetual feelings of guilt. By discovering why God hates divorce (Mal 2:16) she was able to identify and confess for the first time the specific sins she had committed during the marriage. The crushing self-condemnation that had plagued her began to lift. Over time she found fresh grace to forgive—her ex-husband, his attorney, her family, and the church that had rejected her.

Ever since her divorce, Samantha had careened wildly between a paralyzing fear of relationships and obsessive desires for male companionship. While God had graciously spared her from further disastrous relationships, she felt vulnerable to temptation. She also felt different than other singles because she believed they were naive about what marriage was like. As she began to identify herself and her trials biblically she began to see that she was more like her never-married acquaintances than she had imagined. She was able to begin to develop friendships with other single sisters and to relate to single men at work and in the church with a new set of convictions and motivations. She began to experience fellowship and walk in biblical love.

Several months after our initial conversation, Samantha once again sat before me with a troubled expression. "God has been so good to me," she said. "This has been the greatest season of my life. But I've got another question that I'm afraid to ask. I've started to think more and more about whether or not I will ever get married again. It has all of a sudden hit me that maybe I can't! Maybe the Bible does not permit me to re-marry after my divorce. How can you help me figure that out?"

Samantha had stumbled onto what I feel is the great unspoken question of the divorced Christian single. Like a rock lying just below the surface of the waves, the question of whether the Bible will permit a divorced person to remarry is ready to shipwreck the dreams of many divorced Christians. We know God has a place in his plan for divorced Christians. But can that plan ever include the opportunity to marry again? All divorced Christians know it is this question that will most determine their present approach to singleness and their future vision for life in Christ.

Again, I must refrain from giving a particular position here. Our church's position on divorce encompasses this question and the methods we use to deal with it. Most churches with a high regard for Scripture will likewise have a method for approaching these issues. For purposes of this appendix, it is only important to know that the position I personally hold as a pastor is that there are a very few circumstances where divorced people are biblically free to remarry. The complicated issues that often accompany the history of any particular divorce need to be examined carefully in light of the appropriate scriptural truth. Each situation must be judged on its own merits with a view toward God's merciful forgiveness, yet in a way that honors the holiness of God's covenantal nature.

For Samantha, even to pose this question required a great step of faith. "I'd like to tell you about my divorce," she said to me, "and would ask you to judge whether or not I can biblically consider marriage as an option for my future. I am not involved in a relationship, but I don't want to begin to have feelings for someone only to find out that our relationship can never go anywhere. I trust God that he will give you wisdom and I am willing to abide by your decision."

At times like this a pastor can feel the weight of a person's future in his hands. It is a humbling burden. I began to draw out from her all the relevant information I could. At times it was difficult. Some of it involved Samantha confessing shameful things, but it was important to get to the reality of what happened. Samantha knew I would not render this decision alone, but would consult with the rest of the pastoral staff and possibly with other leaders experienced in making these types of judgements. As I studied this matter in Scripture, I was sobered by the words of the writer of Hebrews, "Obey your leaders and submit to their authority. They keep watch over you as men who must give an account" (Heb 13:17). There are few times when greater faith is placed in God's appointed leadership in his church than when a divorced person submits his or her future opportunity for marriage to a pastor. And there are few times when a pastor feels the burden of his accountability before the Lord more keenly than when a divorced person has expressed so bold a trust.

During the season we were deliberating this issue, Samantha learned a great deal about living for the glory of God. She knew she could have easily have found a church that would not raise the issue of her divorce. She also knew she still had the opportunity to disagree with whatever we decided. But she had seen the goodness and mercy of God at work in redeeming her life and her past. She had taken steps of trust and submission to God's pastoral agency for her life in a local church, and had reaped benefits beyond her greatest expectations. How could she now begin to negotiate her obedience to God's truth by avoiding the implications of his Word in the Bible? Radical faith is always identifiable, even if it appears in unlikely places. At this moment, Samantha was radiating radical faith.

After much prayer, study, and counsel, I met with Samantha to tell her our stance. It seemed clear that she had been abandoned in her marriage and that it was appropriate for her to remarry. (Please note that there are not enough details presented here to provide the reader with the basis for our determination.) She was obviously greatly relieved by this. But I'll never forget what she told me through her tears as she left that day.

"You know, I am happy with this news, but somewhere in this process, I stopped hoping for it. For the last couple of weeks I have been content like never before. This whole issue of marriage and divorce and all that—it's no longer a struggle. God really used this waiting period to change my heart regarding singleness. Thank you for not judging me, and for giving me the truth. I am committed to the Lord's way or no way from now on." Samantha was a walking testimony to the power of God. A wandering marriage casualty had been transformed by God's love, God's truth, and God's means into a woman of radical faith.

Where is Samantha today? She is happily married to a wonderful Christian man. She is also contentedly single, serving God, and preparing herself for whenever God might bring his choice into her life. How can this be? Because Samantha's story is the story of many divorced women I have known. There are Sams as well—divorced men whose sense of failure and loss is every bit as profound.

Are you divorced? I would be less than honest if I told you that you won't encounter some significant obstacles in your pursuit of the rich single life. Don't lose heart. Find a church community that takes the needs of the divorced and the standard of truth with equal seriousness. Find what God is doing with your single brothers and sisters and give yourself to it with abandon. There is a place waiting for you in the family of the King. Find it and fill it to the glory of God. ■

NOTES **STUDY ONE – An Excellent Investment**

1. Douglas L. Fagerstrom, ed., *Singles Ministry Handbook* (Wheaton, IL: Victor Books, 1988), p. 26.
2. Ibid., p. 73.
3. Barbara Holland, *One's Company: Reflections on Living Alone* (New York, NY: Ballantine Books, 1992), p. 251.
4. Ibid., p. 6.
5. Quoted by John R.W. Stott, in *The Cross of Christ* (Downers Grove, IL: InterVarsity Press, 1986), p. 45.
6. V.M. Sinton, *New Dictionary of Christian Ethics & Pastoral Theology* (Downers Grove, IL: InterVarsity Press, 1995), p. 790.
7. Elisabeth Elliot, *Let Me Be a Woman* (Wheaton, IL: Tyndale House Publishers, 1976), p. 40.
8. Paige Benton, *Re:generation Quarterly.*
9. John Piper and Wayne Grudem, eds., *Recovering Biblical Manhood and Womanhood* (Wheaton, IL: Crossway Books, 1991), p. xxiii.
10. John Wesley, *The Works of John Wesley,* Volume XI (Albany, OR: The SAGE Digital Library, 1995), p. 540.
11. Randy Alcorn, *Money, Possessions and Eternity* (Wheaton, IL: Tyndale House Publishers, 1989), p. 134.

STUDY TWO – Rich in Identity

1. Carol W. Cornish, in Elyse Fitzpatrick and Carol Cornish, eds., *Women Helping Women* (Eugene, OR: Harvest House Publishers, 1997), p. 72.
2. Douglas L. Fagerstrom, ed., *Singles Ministry Handbook* (Wheaton, IL: Victor Books 1988).
3. Ibid., p. 91.
4. Don Matzat, in Michael Scott Horton, ed., *Power Religion* (Chicago, IL: Moody Press, 1992), p. 258.
5. Mark Altrogge, "A Sinner Who Loves Grace" (1997, People of Destiny International/BMI)
6. Warren W. Wiersbe, *The Best of A.W. Tozer* (Harrisburg, PA: Christian Publications, Inc. 1978), p. 121
7. Bob Bennett, "Lord of the Past" (1989, Matters of the Heart Music/ASCAP)
8. John Bettler, "Counseling and the Problem of the Past," *The Journal of Biblical Counseling,* Vol. XII, No. 2, Winter 1994, p. 14.
9. Edward T. Welch, "Exalting Pain? Ignoring Pain? What Do We Do with Suffering," *The Journal of Biblical Counseling,* Vol. XII, No. 3, Spring 1994, p. 11.
10. Jerry Bridges, *The Discipline of Grace* (Colorado Springs, CO: NavPress 1994), p. 18
11. Charite Lees Bancroft, "Before the Throne of God Above," public domain.
12. John Owen, *Sin and Temptation* (Minneapolis, MN: Bethany House Publishers, 1996) p. 24.
13. Gordon D. Fee, *God's Empowering Presence* (Peabody, MA: Hendrickson Publishers, 1994), p. 433.
14. Jerry Bridges, *The Discipline of Grace* (Colorado Springs, CO: NavPress, 1994), p. 18.
15. Paul Tripp, *The Journal of Biblical Counseling,* Vol. 13, No. 1, Fall 1994, p. 16.
16. Chris Wright, "It's For You" (1995, Here to There Music/ASCAP)

STUDY THREE – Rich in Vision

1. Dee Jepsen, in John Piper and Wayne Grudem, eds.,
   Recovering Biblical Manhood and Womanhood (Wheaton, IL:
   Crossway Books, 1991), p. 388.
2. Randy C. Alcorn, *Christians in the Wake of the Sexual Revolution*
   (Portland, OR: Multnomah Press, 1985), p. 172
3. John Piper, in John Piper and Wayne Grudem, eds.,
   Recovering Biblical Manhood and Womanhood, p. 46.
4. Quoted in *CBMW News*, October 1996.
5. Quoted by Carolyn Warner in *The Last Word* (Englewood Cliffs, NJ:
   Prentice Hall, 1992), p. 40.
6. Quoted in *The Philadelphia Inquirer*, 1/29/97.
7. Quoted in *USA Today*, 5/3/98, p. 20.
8. David Powlison, "Your Looks - What the Voices Say and the Images
   Portray," *The Journal of Biblical Counseling*, Vol. 15, No. 2, Winter
   1997, p. 40.
9. Richard Mayhue in John MacArthur, ed., *Rediscovering Pastoral
   Ministry* (Dallas, TX: Word Publishing, 1995) pp. 160-161.
10. John Angell James, *Female Piety* (Morgan, PA: Soli Deo Gloria
    Publications, 1994), p. 137.
11. Quoted by Carolyn Warner in *The Last Word*, p. 40.
12. Lorrie Skowronski, in Elyse Fitzpatrick and Carol Cornish, eds.
    Women Helping Women (Eugene, OR: Harvest House Publishers,
    1997), p. 145.
13. David Hazard, *You Are My Hiding Place/Amy Carmichael*
    (Minneapolis, MN: Bethany House Publishers, 1991), p. 44.
14. John Piper, in John Piper and Wayne Grudem, eds., *Recovering
    Biblical Manhood and Womanhood,* p. 36.
15. J. Oswald Sanders, *Spiritual Leadership* (Chicago, IL: Moody Press,
    1980), p. 25.
16. Henry T. Blackaby and Claude V. King, *Experiencing God* (Broadman
    & Holman Publishers, 1994), p. 133.
17. Quoted in "Thought for the Week," *Washington Business Journal*
    June 15-21, 1992.
18. Charles Spurgeon, *The Power of Prayer in a Believer's Life*
    (Lunnwood, WA: Emerald Books, 1993), p. 96.
19. Attributed to D.L. Thompson.

STUDY FOUR – Rich in Wisdom

1. J.I. Packer, *Knowing God* (Downers Grove, IL: InterVarsity Press,
   1973), p. 210.
2. Ibid., p. 80.
3. J.I. Packer, *Concise Theology* (Wheaton, IL: Tyndale House
   Publishers, 1993), p. 48
4. J.A. Motyer, *The Bible Speaks Today* (Downers Grove, IL: Inter-
   Varsity Press, 1985), p. 39.
5. Romans 11:33-36.
6. Wayne Grudem, *Systematic Theology* (Grand Rapids, MI: Zondervan
   Publishing House, 1994), p. 193.
7. *New Bible Dictionary* (Downers Grove, IL: Inter-Varsity Press, 1962),
   p. 1244.
8. John Wesley, *The Works of John Wesley,* Volume XI (Albany, OR: The
   SAGE Digital Library, 1995), p. 320.
9. John Calvin, *Institutes of the Christian Religion* (Albany, OR: The
   SAGE Digital Library, 1996), p. 55.

10. John Calvin, *Institutes of the Christian Religion*, p. 659.
11. Quoted by Sinclair B. Ferguson in *Discovering God's Will* (Carlisle, PA: Banner of Truth, 1982), p. 45.
12. Sinclair B. Ferguson in *Discovering God's Will* (Carlisle, PA: Banner of Truth, 1982).
13. John Piper, *Future Grace* (Sisters, OR: Multnomah Books, 1995), p. 242.
14. Quoted by J.I. Packer in *A Quest for Godliness* (Wheaton, IL: Crossway Books, 1990), p. 95.
15. Bruce Milne, Introduction to *Know the Truth* (Downers Grove, IL: Inter-Varsity Press, 1982).
16. Matt Redman, "The Friendship and the Fear," (1997, ThankYou Music)
17. Dallas Willard, *The Spirit of the Disciplines* (New York, NY: HarperCollins Publishers, 1988), p. 261.
18. Donald S. Whitney, *Spiritual Disciplines for the Christian Life* (Colorado Springs, CO: NavPress, 1991), p. 18.
19. Jack Deere, *Surprised by the Voice of God* (Grand Rapids, MI: Zondervan Publishing House, 1996), p. 117.
20. Bruce Waltke, *Finding the Will of God* (Gresham, OR; Vision House Publishing, 1995), p. 35.
21. Wayne Martindale and Jerry Root, eds., *The Quotable Lewis* (Wheaton, IL: Tyndale House Publishers, 1989), p. 233
22. J.C. Ryle, *The Duties of Parents* (Conrad, MT: Triangle Press, 1994), p. 12.
23. Vinita Hampton Wright and Mary Horner, *Women's Wisdom Through the Ages* (Wheaton, IL: Harold Shaw Publishers, 1994), p. 12.
24. John Piper, *Future Grace*, p. 171.
25. Dallas Willard, *In Search of Guidance* (New York, NY: Harper Collins, 1993), p. 220.
26. Jerry Bridges, *Trusting God* (Colorado Springs, CO: NavPress, 1988), p. 170.

STUDY FIVE – Rich in Impact
1. R.C. Sproul, *Pleasing God* (Wheaton, IL: Tyndale House Publishers, 1988), pp. 57, 59.
2. James B. Twitchell, *AdCult USA* (New York, NY: Columbia University Press, 1996).
3. Randy C. Alcorn, *Money, Possessions and Eternity* (Wheaton, IL: Tyndale House Publishers, 1989), p. 415.
4. *Newsweek*, October 20, 1997, p. 56.
5. D. Martyn Lloyd-Jones, *Life in the Spirit* (Grand Rapids, MI: Baker Book House, 1973), p. 315.
6. Oswald Chambers, *My Utmost for His Highest* (Grand Rapids, MI: Discovery House, 1963) p. 332.
7. Henry T. Blackaby and Claude V. King, *Experiencing God* (Broadman & Holman Publishers, 1994), pp. 93-4.
8. Robert Grant, *Christ's Kingdom in the Marketplace*, p. 24.
9. D.A. Carson, *A Call to Spiritual Reformation* (Grand Rapids, MI: Baker Book House, 1992).
10. Quoted in Harold Ivan Smith, *A Singular Devotion* (Old Tappan, NJ: Fleming H. Revell, 1990), p. 52.
11. William White in Douglas L. Fagerstrom, ed., *Singles Ministry Handbook* (Wheaton, IL: Victor Books, 1988), p. 75.

12. Joshua Harris, "Scream the Dream," *Sovereign Grace*, Sept/Oct 1997, p. 13.

13. Martin Luther King, *The Words of Martin Luther King, Jr.* (New York, NY: Newmarket Press, 1987), p. 17

14. Leland Ryken, *Redeeming the Time* (Grand Rapids, MI: Baker Book House Company, 1995), p. 272.

15. William Law, *A Serious Call to a Devout and Holy Life* (Albany, OR: The SAGE Digital Library, 1996), p. 36.

16. Margaret Clarkson, *So You're Single!* (Wheaton, IL: Harold Shaw Publishers, 1978), p. 21.

17. John Piper, *Future Grace* (Sisters, OR: Multnomah Books, 1995), p. 258.

18. Charles Spurgeon, *A Good Start* (Morgan, PA: Soli Deo Gloria Publications, 1995), p. 309.

STUDY SIX – Rich in Relationships (I): Investing in Friendship

1. Quoted by William J. Bennett in *The Book of Virtues* (New York, NY: Simon & Schuster, 1993), p. 329.

2. *SAM Journal*, Sep/Oct 1996, p. 1.

3. Quoted by William J. Bennett in *The Book of Virtues*, p. 331.

4. Margaret Clarkson, *So You're Single!* (Wheaton, IL: Harold Shaw Publishers, 1978), p. 75, 85.

5. Quoted by Mark Shaw in *Ten Great Ideas from Church History* (Downers Grove, IL: InterVarsity Press, 1997), p. 209.

6. Eugene H. Peterson, *The Message* (Colorado Springs, CO: NavPress, 1993), pp. 359-60.

7. Jonathan Edwards, *A Treatise Concerning Religious Affections*, (Albany, OR: The SAGE Digital Library, 1996), p. 342.

8. *New Dictionary of Christian Ethics & Pastoral Theology* (Downers Grove, IL: InterVarsity Press, 1995), p. 379.

9. John Loftness in C.J. Mahaney, ed., *Why Small Groups?* (Gaithersburg, MD: PDI Communications, 1996), p. 22.

10. Quoted by Jerry Bridges in *The Crisis of Caring* (Colorado Springs, CO: NavPress, 1985), pp. 80-1.

11. Charles Haddon Spurgeon, *The Spurgeon Sermon Collection* (Albany, OR: The SAGE Digital Library, 1996), p. 472.

12. J.C. Ryle, *Thoughts for Young Men* (Amityville, NY: Calvary Press, 1996), p. 57.

13. Wayne Martindale and Jerry Root, eds., *The Quotable Lewis* (Wheaton, IL: Tyndale House Publishers, 1989), p. 238.

14. Thomas à Kempis, *The Imitation of Christ* (Albany, OR: The SAGE Digital Library, 1996), p. 22.

15. Quoted in *Sovereign Grace,* July/August 1997, p. 3.

16. Twila Paris, "True Friend," (Ariose Music/ASCAP, 1988)

17. John Wesley, *The Works of John Wesley* (Albany, OR: The SAGE Digital Library, 1995), p. 74.

18. 1 John 1:5-9.

19. Ken Sande, *The Peacemaker* (Grand Rapids, MI: Baker Book House, 1991), p. 22.

20. Ibid., p. 170.

STUDY SEVEN – Rich in Relationships (II): Courting Relationships

1. Joshua Harris, *I Kissed Dating Goodbye* (Sisters, OR: Multnomah Books, 1997), p. 24.

2. Douglas J. Wilson, *Her Hand in Marriage* (Moscow, ID: Canon Press, 1997), p. 10.
3. *Swing,* May 1997, p. 85.
4. *U.S. News & World Report*, 5/19/97, p. 58.
5. Douglas J. Wilson, *Her Hand in Marriage*, p. 85
6. Elisabeth Elliot, *Quest for Love* (Grand Rapids, MI: Baker Book House, 1996), p. 203.
7. Wayne Martindale and Jerry Root, eds., *The Quotable Lewis* (Wheaton, IL: Tyndale House Publishers, 1989), p. 403.
8. Randy C. Alcorn, *Christians in the Wake of the Sexual Revolution* (Portland, OR: Multnomah Press, 1985), p. 221.
9. Andrew Swanson, *Whom Shall I Marry?* (Carlisle, PA; Banner of Truth, 1995), p. 29.
10. Jeffery S. Forrey, "Biblical Counsel for Concerned Singles," *The Journal of Biblical Counseling*, Vol. 14, No. 3, Spring 1996, p. 31.

STUDY EIGHT – Rich Toward Marriage
1. *Philadelphia Inquirer*, 3/21/93.
2. James Patterson and Peter Kim, *The Day America Told the Truth* (Englewood Cliffs, NJ: Prentice Hall, 1991), p.88.
3. Ruthe Stein, *The Art of Single Living* (New York, NY: Shapolsky Publishers, 1990).
4. R.C. Sproul, *Discovering the Intimate Marriage* (Minneapolis, MN: Bethany Fellowship, 1975), pp. 120-1.
5. John Stott, *Authentic Christianity* (Downers Grove, IL: InterVarsity Press, 1995), p. 373.
6. A.A. Hodge, *The Confession of Faith* (Simpsonville, SC: Christian Classics Foundation, 1997), p. 1.
7. John Piper, "Perspectives on Family," *CBMW News*, October 1996, p. 13.
8. Vinita Hampton Wright and Mary Horner, *Women's Wisdom Through the Ages* (Wheaton, IL: Harold Shaw Publishers, 1994), p. 90.
9. Elisabeth Elliot, *Loneliness* (Nashville, TN: Oliver-Nelson Books, 1988), p. 57.
10. Quoted by J.B. McClure in *Pearls from Many Seas* (Albany, OR: The SAGE Digital Library, 1995), p. 312.
11. Wayne Martindale and Jerry Root, eds., *The Quotable Lewis* (Wheaton, IL: Tyndale House Publishers, 1989), p. 412.
12. Quoted by J.I. Packer in *A Quest for Godliness* (Wheaton, IL: Good News Publishers, 1990), p. 263.

STUDY NINE – Rich in Hope
1. *New Dictionary of Christian Ethics & Pastoral Theology* (Downers Grove, IL: InterVarsity Press, 1995), p. 557.
2. Quoted by Carolyn Warner in *The Last Word* (Englewood Cliffs, NJ: Prentice Hall, 1992), p. 136
3. Margaret Clarkson, *So You're Single!* (Wheaton, IL: Harold Shaw Publishers, 1978), p. 135.
4. Dallas Willard, *In Search of Guidance* (New York, NY: HarperCollins Publishers, 1993), p. 39.
5. J. Oswald Sanders, *Facing Loneliness* (Grand Rapids, MI: Discovery House, 1990), p. 122.
6. Charles Haddon Spurgeon, *The Spurgeon Sermon Collection* (Albany, OR: The SAGE Digital Library, 1996), p. 854

7. Paul Tripp, "Keeping Destiny in View," *The Journal of Biblical Counseling*, Vol. 13, No. 1, Fall 1994, p. 21.

8. Elisabeth Elliot, *Loneliness* (Nashville, TN: Oliver-Nelson Books, 1988), p. 127.

9. Quoted by Leslie K. Tarr in "The Story of John Bunyan: Progress of a Pilgrim", *Decision,* September 1988, p. 14, 30.

10. John Angell James, *Female Piety* (Morgan, PA: Soli Deo Gloria Publications, 1994), pp. 264-5.

11. Romans 5:15.

12. John Calvin, *Institutes of the Christian Religion* (Albany, OR: The SAGE Digital Library, 1996), pp. 676-7.

13. Dan Haseltine, "Like A Child," (Bridge Building Music/BMI, Pogostick Music/BMI, 1995)

14. *Compassion*, Fall/Winter 1995, p. 27.

15. Warren W. Wiersbe, *The Best of A.W. Tozer* (Harrisburg, PA: Baker Book House, 1978), pp. 198-9.

16. Randy C. Alcorn, *Money, Possessions and Eternity* (Wheaton, IL: Tyndale House Publishers, 1989), p. 201.

17. Isaac Watts, "O God Our Help in Ages Past," public domain.

OTHER TITLES IN PDI'S *PURSUIT OF GODLINESS* SERIES

DISCIPLINED FOR LIFE   John Loftness and C.J. Mahaney

Are you satisfied with the depth of your devotional life? If you're like most Christians, probably not. *Disciplined for Life* puts change within your grasp. Leave the treadmill of spiritual drudgery behind as you discover fresh motivation and renewed passion to practice the spiritual disciplines. (112 pages)

THIS GREAT SALVATION   Robin Boisvert and C.J. Mahaney

Countless Christians struggle through life feeling condemned and confused. No matter how much they do for God, they never feel quite sure of his acceptance. Sound at all familiar? Then you'll find *great* news in *This Great Salvation*. Start enjoying a new measure of grace and peace at every level of your Christian life as this unique book reveals all God has done for you through Christ. (112 pages)

HOW CAN I CHANGE?   Robin Boisvert and C.J. Mahaney

How Can I Change? (originally titled *From Glory to Glory*) rests on a remarkable assumption: If you will study and apply the doctrine of sanctification, any sin can be overcome. Have you known the frustration of falling short in your efforts to please God? Have you questioned whether you will *ever* be able to change? If so, this book will have a profound impact on your walk with Christ. (112 pages)

LOVE THAT LASTS   Gary and Betsy Ricucci

A magnificent marriage is more than wishful thinking. It can and should be the experience of every husband and wife willing to follow God's plan for them as a couple. Whether your marriage is new, needy, or simply ready for a refresher, here is an excellent guide for helping you build a thriving, lasting love. (176 pages)

WALKING WITH THE WISE   Benny and Sheree Phillips

At last…a book to keep your hopes and standards high during the adolescent years! Written for parents and teens to use together, *Walking with the Wise* hits the "big issues" such as dating, peer pressure, and passion for God. Reinforce your relationship and strengthen your convictions with this valuable resource for parents and teens. (192 pages)

FIRST STEPS OF FAITH   Steve Shank

Other than a Bible, what's the first resource you would give a brand-new Christian? *First Steps of Faith* will meet that critical need. Using vivid, personal illustrations, Steve Shank lays a solid yet simple foundation for a lifetime of growth. Mature Christians will also find plenty of meat as they explore the attributes of God, our battle against indwelling sin, and much more. (112 pages)

WHY SMALL GROUPS?   C.J. Mahaney, General Editor

Not simply a how-to guide, this illuminating book starts by answering the all-important question of *why* a church needs small groups. The short answer? Because small groups are invaluable in helping us to "work out our salvation together" in practical, biblical ways. Specially developed for leaders and members of small groups alike, *Why Small Groups?* is loaded with insight, wisdom, and practical instruction. This book can put you on the fast track to Christian maturity. (144 pages)

ADDITIONAL RESOURCES FROM PDI COMMUNICATIONS

PRAISE AND WORSHIP MUSIC

PDI worship songs have been in use for more than a decade in local churches around the world. By the grace and mercy of God, more than 10,000 churches in the United States alone currently use these Christ-centered, Cross-centered songs to worship and glorify God. PDI Music's *Come and Worship* series features two releases per year.

> "PDI's music has passion, prophetic insight, and vision.
> I strongly recommend it to local churches everywhere."
> **Stuart Townend, songwriter, worship leader, and Head of Kingsway Music**

> "These songs are vital, rich, and heart-probing...
> PDI music moves my heart to worship."
> **Randy Alcorn, author of *Edge of Eternity, Deadline*, and**
> ***Money, Possessions and Eternity***

> "If I could only have one source for new songs, I'd choose PDI."
> **Tom Kraeuter, former Managing Editor, *Psalmist Magazine* and author of**
> ***Worship is...What?***

TEACHING TAPES

Powerful messages on a wide variety of topics. Thousands have been evangelized, exhorted, encouraged, and instructed by these taped messages.

SOVEREIGN GRACE MAGAZINE

In circulation for more than 17 years, this bi-monthly publication addresses the most critical issues facing Christians today. It also profiles the people and progress of PDI's team-related churches in the United States and abroad.

For a catalog of PDI resources and a free issue of *Sovereign Grace*, call **1-800-736-2202** or write to us:

PDI Communications
7881 Beechcraft Avenue, Suite B
Gaithersburg, MD 20879
Attention: Resource Center

pdi@pdinet.org
fax: 301-948-7833
www.pdinet.org